A Practical
Guide
to
Affiliate
Marketing

A Practical Guide to Affiliate Marketing

to

Affiliate

Marketing

Quick Reference for Affiliate Managers & Merchants

Evgenii "Geno" Prussakov

A Practical Guide to Affiliate Marketing
Copyright © 2007 by Evgenii Prussakov

Library of Congress Cataloging-in-Publication Data

Prussakov, Evgenii
    A Practical Guide to Affiliate Marketing / Evgenii Prussakov

ISBN-10: 0-9791927-0-6
ISBN-13: 978-0-9791927-0-8

Printed in the United States of America

To Lena
My faithful friend and loving wife,
whose support and encouragement have been essential
components of all my affiliate marketing endeavors.

Contents

3. Pro Level

Part 2: AFFILIATE MANAGER & MERCHANT MISTAKES

APPENDIX

Acknowledgements

Many have helped me in getting this book ready for publication. First, I would like to thank Haiko de Poel, Jr. for his encouragement in this project, as well as for providing the world with ABestWeb.com – an excellent affiliate and merchant educational platform. For offering their constructive criticism upon reading this manuscript, my thanks go to Brian Littleton of ShareASale, Kellie Stevens of AffiliateFairPlay.com, Mal Cowley of buy.at, and Chris Sanderson of AMWSO. For all her hours spent in front of the computer proofreading, I am grateful to my dear friend, Gina Alexander. But most of all, no one has given up more, nor had more of a share in this accomplishment than my wife, Lena. Her patience and support in helping me to get this manuscript written and published cannot be underestimated. Finally, my little Princess Anastasia – who turned three while I was writing this book – involuntarily sacrificed countless hours of play with her father and should definitely be mentioned here as well.

Introduction

The book you hold in your hands is written to satisfy the obvious demand for a practical guide to affiliate marketing. The idea of writing this book stems back to the years I myself have spent learning about affiliate programs, about the way they work, and systematizing this knowledge. I only wish a book such as this was available back when I first started. It would have simplified many things for me personally, not to mention for all those who, up until now, have had to look for answers in dozens of different places. I wanted to create a book that could be referred to easily for accurate and practical information.

This creation of mine is mainly aimed at two categories of readers: *merchants* and *affiliate managers*. The former category includes all those that are either considering starting an affiliate program or already have one running, while the latter one embraces both new and more experienced affiliate managers. Most of the book is geared towards the beginning affiliate managers, yet those who are more savvy will also find a good portion of material that is useful to them. Much of what is presented on the following pages has been learned through trial-and-error – by making mistakes. These mistakes, and the lessons they teach, come to you from my own personal experience. I also share mistakes made by other affiliate managers – mistakes which have come to my attention through many other affiliates and managers, alike. As the wise old saying goes: "learn from the mistakes of others." You will find over a hundred of them in the pages that follow.

To simplify its use, I have arranged the material of this book into three parts:

1) Questions & Answers
2) Affiliate Manager & Merchant Mistakes
3) Ideas for Affiliate Program Promotion

The first part of the book represents 70 questions and answers about affiliate marketing and affiliate programs, and is categorized into three groups: (i) questions pertaining to the consideration of starting an affiliate program, (ii) questions that arise when one has already decided to start a program, and (iii) questions that one has to face when an affiliate program is already started and practical management issues are confronted. It is worth mentioning that since the book is geared at two groups whose interests may differ at times (merchants and affiliate managers), some of the questions (e.g.: "Do I need to hire an affiliate manager?" or "How much should I pay my affiliate manager?") should be read keeping in mind that they were written for one group of readers (in this case, merchants). I believe, however, that answers to merchants' questions may at times be extremely helpful to affiliate managers, and visa versa.

The second part of this book lists 100 actual errors affiliate managers and merchants routinely commit. Frankly speaking, I would recommend every affiliate manager study them, regardless of his/her experience. These are also arranged in three groups: (i) those errors committed within an affiliate program, (ii) those that you want to avoid within the website that runs an affiliate program, and (iii) the mistakes you want to avoid making in your day-to-day affiliate program management.

I have tried to refer to practical cases throughout the book, giving applicable pieces of advice on all of the topics covered.

The third part of the book embodies 30 practical ideas on affiliate program promotion. I hope you will find them helpful, and that you will be able to use them to take your affiliate program management to new heights.

4

When reading the book you may run across unknown abbreviations and acronyms. For the most part, they are widely accepted throughout the Internet marketing sphere in general, and in the affiliate marketing field in particular. When an abbreviation is used in this book, it should not be unknown to you if you are reading the book from the start. Each term is defined in full before its abbreviation is used. If, however, you are reading the book selectively – following the table of contents – you may run into unknown shortenings. In this case, please use the list of "Internet Marketing Acronyms & Abbreviations" at the end of the book.

Part 1
Questions & Answers

1
Pre-Launch Phase

Q.: What is affiliate marketing?

A.: One of the greatest of all French authors, François-Marie Arouet de Voltaire said: "If you wish to converse with me, define your terms". Let me follow the philosopher's advice at the very outset of this book.

Affiliate marketing is basically performance-based marketing, whereby affiliates/partners promote a merchant's product/service and get remunerated for every sale, visit, or subscription sent to the merchant. The most frequently used payment arrangements include: pay-per-sale, pay-per-lead, and pay-per-click compensations. Affiliate marketing is one of the most powerful and effective customer acquisition tools available to an online merchant today. You decide what commission to pay, and pay only when results (sales, leads and/or clicks) are obvious.

Affiliate marketing owes its birth and first developments to CDNow.com and Amazon.com. Back in November, 1994 CDNow started its Buyweb Program – the first online marketing program of its kind at that time. Amazon continued this pattern in July 1996 with its Associates Program. Amazon claims that currently the number of their affiliates worldwide exceeds 1 million associates.

Q.: Is an affiliate program a viable marketing option for my business?

A.: Any online business will surely be enhanced by running an affiliate program. Since the essence of affiliate marketing is in placing the main emphasis on the actual sale occurred, it is always a no-lose situation for the merchant (unless you pay for clicks or leads, of course). When starting an affiliate program you may decide to remunerate affiliates for clicks sent to you. This is only one option. In fact, most affiliate programs do *not*. Most merchants tie the compensation of affiliates solely to the registered and

11

confirmed sales (fraudulent, duplicate, and other invalid sales do not count). Check what your competition is doing. Chances are that upon querying any major search engine by using a "<your product> affiliate program" key-phrase, it will be much easier for you to answer this question as it pertains to your own business.

Q.: Does affiliate marketing work for one-product stores?

A.: It does. It is not about how many different products you have featured at your website, but always about the uniqueness of the product itself, the attractiveness of its characteristics, and the persuasion of the selling point. Yes, affiliates tend to like multi-product retail-type online stores better, but by no means does this indicate that a one-product or a one-service online business is "unmarketable" via the affiliate channel. If you hesitate, hire an affiliate marketing consultant to advise you on the sellability of your product through affiliates. But do not turn away from the possibility – one that could grow into an opportunity to enhance the capabilities of your online business – before you have fully done your homework.

Q.: Does it work for one-of-a-kind products?

A.: Does a one-of-a-kind concept work for you when you sell your product(s) at your own website? Of course it does. Uniqueness and exclusivity are always excellent selling points. In the beginning it may be harder for you to recruit affiliates with relevant traffic, but once you have convinced your affiliates that your product really sells, they will more than likely give it a try. Overstock.com has a "Worldstock Handcrafted" section at their website, and these limited-quantity products sell very well for them. You will need to provide your affiliates with good creative and link support, but isn't this a "must" for any affiliate program that wants to succeed? Yes, your product will sell through the affiliate marketing channel, but you may need to do some preliminary affiliate educating in the starting phases of your affiliate program.

Q.: How does one get started?

A.: To plug into the affiliate marketing world you need to start an affiliate program. An affiliate program can be launched either on an affiliate network or with in-house software (which can either be bought or built).

Q.: What are the startup costs?

A.: Starting an affiliate program, either in-house or on a network, is generally reasonable. Options start from a few hundred US dollars.

Q.: What is an affiliate program?

A.: An affiliate program is a business arrangement whereby one party (the merchant) agrees to pay another party (the affiliate) a referral fee or commission. This fee/commission is paid for all the sales that occur in the event of the end customer clicking the affiliate link which leads to the merchant's website, and thus, results in a purchase. Sometimes a clarification is made that the commission is paid on all *confirmed* orders.

Affiliate programs are also called associate, reseller, commission, revenue-sharing, bounty, or partnership programs. The payment pattern may sometimes also be reflected in the way they are called, being referred to as pay-per-lead, pay-per-sale, or pay-for-performance programs.

Q.: May affiliate expenses substitute my other online marketing expenses?

A.: They may, and it is up to you how to budget this. The following statistics may be of help. Nielsen//NetRatings 2005-2006 reports show that the top 10 online retailer's conversion rates fluctuate between 12% and 16%. The list includes such giant online businesses as Yahoo! Shopping, eBay, Amazon, L.L. Bean, and QVC. Small and medium-sized online businesses (SMOB's) face much more dismal results in conversion of browsers into buyers. The average customer conversion rate is registered only at about 2.5%.

As for the affiliate marketing channel, one of Shawn Collins' studies shows that 18% of marketers see their conversion rates on affiliate marketing programs at 0.5-1%, 14% of respondents cite rates greater than 5%, and another 16% say they do not know the conversion rate. My better performing affiliate programs convert at a 7.5+% rate, which is undoubtedly better than that 2.5% mark for the average customer conversion rate in SMOB's statistics.

Would it then be sensible to cease all of your other online marketing efforts, focusing solely on affiliate marketing, and investing your entire marketing budget into it? It may be, but I would recommend taking it one step at a time. The first thing I would cut off is most of your banner advertising (if you are running any such campaigns). Secondly, unless you are a PPC expert yourself, I would look into recruiting quality PPC affiliates, narrowing my PPC campaigns only to those keywords that convert best. Then let PPC affiliates use their experience and expertise to send you more PPC traffic and sales. Take it one step at a time, and you may very well free up some of your marketing resources (both time and money implied), to invest into affiliate marketing.

Q.: What time investment are we talking about?

A.: It may take as little as 1-1.5 hours a day, or as much a full working day four to five days a week. Outsourced affiliate managers normally commit to between 40 and 80 hours a month, which, when divided by the number of work days in a given month, results in anywhere between 2 and 4 hours a day. If you decide to run the affiliate program yourself, your time management will be entirely in your hands. If you do choose to run it yourself, set aside about 1.5-2 hours a day during the first two months for study, plus roughly 1 hour a day for the application of what you have learned. Starting from month three you may cut the study time to half an hour a day, and management time to as long as is required by the circumstances, but no less than 40-45 minutes a day.

Q.: Do I need to get additionally certified/educated to run an affiliate program?

A.: Certification is not necessary, and, frankly speaking, currently there is no unified certification accepted across the industry. Some companies, such as Andy Rodriguez Consulting in the USA, and e-Consultancy by Keith Budden in the UK, run seminars on affiliate program management. These last anywhere from one day to a weekend and are extremely informative and practical. Attending a seminar will undoubtedly enrich you as an affiliate manager, as well as help you in the networking aspect of the business. You may also attend affiliate conferences, summits, and other relevant events that will help you grow in your knowledge and increase the list of your contacts in the industry.

While certification is not necessary, educating yourself is a *must*. If you are working on a tight budget, you may not be able to afford attending the above-mentioned events right from the start. Do not despair! You may learn a lot from public affiliate forums (ABestWeb.com being the leading one in the US, and A4Uforum.co.uk, its British counterpart), books on Internet and affiliate marketing, "Revenue" magazine (the industry's only magazine), relevant broadcasts, and research articles published online. Do not let a day pass without learning something new. Sir Francis Bacon stressed: "Knowledge is power", while Margaret Fuller wrote: "If you have knowledge, let others light their candles at it." If you do not heed these wise words, you will undoubtedly find yourself and your affiliate program to be wandering in the dark.

Q.: What are affiliates?

A.: Sometimes also called associates or partners, they are essentially the sales force for your affiliate program. I like to think of affiliates as dealers, or your most valuable partners that promote your brand and your business, investing their own money to sell your product/service.

Q.: What are sub-affiliates?

A.: They are your second tier affiliates, or affiliates that have joined your program by a referral from an affiliate you already have on board your program. Some affiliate programs choose to pay both the sub-affiliate and the affiliate that sent him/her to you on first and second-tier commission basis. We will look into the pros and cons of such a setup a bit later, after we have defined the basics.

Q.: What number of online businesses have affiliate programs?

A.: When launching my client recruitment campaign in the beginning of 2006, I was utterly surprised to see that about 80% of online businesses do not have an affiliate program! Does this mean they do not work? Not at all. On the contrary, my business experience shows differently. Affiliate programs do work, however, many online merchants are simply uneducated about affiliate marketing. Look at the bigger merchants: Amazon, Apple Store, Boscov's, Circuit City, CompUSA, Eddie Bauer, Gateway, Home Depot, HP Home & Office, Magazines.com, NASCAR.com, Overstock.com, Philips, Radio Shack, and Wal-Mart, to name only a few. They all have this in common: they have gigantic affiliate operations in place.

You may think: "The fact that such sharks of the business can afford it does not mean that it will work for me". Oh, let me tell you that it does! Simply do what I have suggested above: type in a "<your product> affiliate program" phrase in any major search engine, and you will see which of your competitors are already doing it. More than likely, you will find out that the number of those utilizing this powerful marketing option is not that large. That is good news. The smaller the number of competitors with affiliate programs in place, the better it is for you. Finish reading the rest of this book and get on it!

Q.: Wouldn't an affiliate commission budget make me noncompetitive?

A.: It shouldn't if you are dealing with the right suppliers and your initial prices are competitive. You may or may not have to increase your prices. Do a quick competitive analysis of those affiliate programs that are already being run in your vertical. See what they are offering to affiliates in terms of the commissions and the cookie life. Then study the "What should the base commission rate be?" question below, and see at what level you can afford to set your commission rate. While doing all of this, remember that more competitive merchant prices, coupled with lower affiliate commissions (than those offered by the less competitive merchants), are normally favored by affiliates much more than the opposite combination (noncompetitive prices with higher commissions). Experience proves that more competitive merchants always convert better, and conversion is one of the *main* factors affiliates look at.

Additionally, do remember that unlike it is with other channels of distribution, the affiliate marketing one hardly has any advertising and marketing expenses, yet often showing the best ROI. You only pay for performance. With most other advertising you get no guarantee and results usually aren't as good.

Q.: How soon will I start seeing sales?

A.: This depends on many factors, including your affiliate manager's contacts and recruitment activity, as well as your brand's popularity and overall website conversion (which is certainly tied to the uniqueness of your proposal to customers). Perhaps you are looking for a more concrete answer than this, so I can tell you the time frame is anywhere from one to two months (depending on how the program is managed).

Q.: What volume of sales should I expect?

A.: This is obviously tied to the sales volume you are already experiencing, but a medium-size business may realistically expect approximately a 10% sales growth after the introduction of an affiliate program. This growth may be expected within the first few months of actively running the program (read:"announcing, promoting, and recruiting"). One of the programs I manage is producing 25% of the business' sales from January through September, and over 45% of the company's gross sales from October through December each year. Such volume was achieved after running the program for under one year.

Q.: What are my options as far as tracking solutions?

A.: If you opt to use an affiliate network, you do not need to worry about sales/visits tracking or manually cutting payments to your affiliates, as the network performs these tasks for you. For their services, networks charge either a percentage of what you pay your affiliates, a flat monthly fee, or a combination of both. If you decide to run your program in-house, you would need to obtain tracking software, hosted services, or a shopping cart with affiliate features. Running reports and paying your affiliates would then be done by you alone.

Q.: What exactly is an affiliate network?

A.: Affiliate networks are essentially mediators connecting affiliates with affiliate programs, providing tracking and maintenance services to the latter. They are sometimes also called "affiliate solution providers" (ASP's), as no additional software is required for the merchant to start and run an affiliate program if they decide to use an affiliate network.

Q.: What affiliate networks are available?

A.: Affiliate networks are numerous. Below you will find a list I have put together. The list arranges affiliate networks strictly in an alphabetical order, not necessarily in order of any personal preference. It is also not my goal to publish a comprehensive list of affiliate networks. What I have done is my best to bring to you the major US, UK, and European networks currently in operation:

USA-Based Affiliate Networks:

Advertising.com (USA)
AffiliateFuel
AffiliateFuture.com

19

AvantLink
ClickBank
ClickBooth
ClickXChange
ClixGalore
CommissionJunction
DarkBlue
DigitalGrit
Incentaclick
Kolimbo
LeadHound.com
LinkConnector
LinkShare
MaxBounty
NetShopsAffiliates.com
PartnerWeekly
Performics
Quinstreet
Rextopia
SaleFlurry
ShareASale
ShareResults
Trade Doubler
Traffic System
TrafficSynergy
Zanox.com

UK-Based Affiliate Networks:

Advertising.com UK
AffiliateFuture.co.uk
AffiliateWindow
Afform
Buy.at
CommissionJunction UK
dhmPerformance (by Deal Group Media)
Netklix
Ocean Affiliates
OMGUK.com

Paid on Results
PrimeQ
UKaffiliates
Webgains.com
Zanox.co.uk
Trade Doubler UK

European Affiliate Networks

AdButler.de (Germany)
Advertising.com (Germany, France, Spain, Denmark, Norway, Sweden)
Affili.net (Germany)
CommissionJunction.de (Germany)
Commission Junction France (France)
Commission Junction Sverige (Sweden)
Zanox CZ (Czech Republic)

Each network has its own rules, regulations, and terms of service. If you are considering starting an affiliate program on a US network and are under a considerable time constraint, I would recommend that you at least look into such networks (again, in alphabetical order only) as AvantLink, CommissionJunction, Google Affiliate Network (formerly DoubleClick Performics), LinkShare, and ShareASale. In the United Kingdom, consider AffiliateFuture.co.uk, Buy.at and PaidOnResults.

Q.: Why pay a network when you can do it all in-house?

A.: From first glance, it may seem to be more effective to run an affiliate program in-house. There are pros and cons to both methods of running an affiliate marketing program. In-house affiliate programs help you save money on network fees, while network-based affiliate programs allow for a broader exposure to an already-existing base of affiliates. It also allows for numerous affiliate recruitment opportunities.

As mentioned above, networks also take away the burden of check-writing, banner serving, reporting, and affiliate technical support. However, some networks spell it out in their TOS that the relationship with all affiliates is property of the networks (regardless of the fact that many of your own affiliates will be recruited by you, personally). The advantages and disadvantages of having a program on the network or running it in-house must be carefully weighed, and the decision be made according to your individual need.

Q.: What in-house software solutions are available to me?

A.: There are quite a few affiliate management software applications out there. Some are hosted at third-party servers, others are script-based, while yet others can be hosted at the merchant's server. Below you will find a fairly full list of the in-house software solutions currently available. Numerous e-commerce solutions and shopping carts now have affiliate tracking features. I am hereby listing a very few – only those that I believe are worth looking at in a section such as this.

1ShoppingCart	www.1shoppingcart.com
Affiliate Clicks	www.affiliateclicks.com
Affiliate Network Pro	www.alstrasoft.com/affiliate.htm
Aff Planet	www.affplanet.com
Affiliate Pro	
	www.regnow.com/softsell/nph-softsell.cgi?item=14111-1
Affiliate Runner	www.affiliaterunner.com
Affiliate Shop	www.affiliateshop.com
Affiliate Tracking	www.affiliatetracking.com
Affiliate Traction	www.affiliatetraction.com
Affiliate Wiz	www.affiliatewiz.com
AShop Deluxe	www.ashopsoftware.com
AssocTRAC	
	www.marketingtips.com/assoctrac/index.html
DigiAffiliate	www.digiappz.com/digiaffiliate.asp

DirectTrack   www.directtrack.com
Fusion Quest   www.fusionquest.com
iDevAffiliate   www.idevdirect.com
Interneka   www.interneka.com
JROX Affiliate Manager jam.jrox.com
JV Manager   www.jvmanager.com/index.shtml
Leadhound   www.leadhoundnetwork.com
Managed Affiliate Programs
     www.managedaffiliateprograms.com
MPA3   www.mpa3.com
MyAffiliateProgram   www.myaffiliateprogram.com
MyReferer   www.myreferer.com
OSI Affiliate   www.osiaffiliate.com
PayDotCom   www.paydotcom.com
Post Affiliate Pro   www.qualityunit.com/postaffiliatepro
QualityClick   www.qc3.de   (for German-speakers)
Synergyx   www.synergyx.com
TWSC Affiliate Lite   www.twsc.biz
Ultimate Affiliate   www.groundbreak.com
X-Affiliate
     www.x-cart.com/affiliate_program.html
Yahoo! Merchant Solutions Track Links
     help.yahoo.com/l/us/yahoo/smallbusiness/store/promote/tools/tools-07.html

If time does not allow you to analyze all of the above, but you still want to consider going in-house, look at such options as DirectTrack, iDevAffiliate, MyAP, and Ultimate Affiliate.

Alert: I normally recommend staying away from the free or inexpensive solutions (under $95.00). Also be careful with free plug-ins for shopping carts. They are not 100% safe and serious affiliates would much rather have you go with either a tried and trusted software, or with one of the major affiliate networks.

Q.: How exactly does one remunerate affiliates?

A.: As an example, let us use a business running retail operations online. Two variables need to be set within the affiliate program: commission structure/model and cookie life. The commission model more commonly used for online stores is the pay-per-sale method, meaning you pay your affiliate a percentage of each sale that he/she sends your way. Rates range from 2% to 50% depending on the industry and the profit margins of the business. Commission is normally credited to the affiliate's account at the moment of sale, but may be reversed if, for some reason, the sale doesn't go through.

Q.: What are cookies and why are they important?

A.: Affiliate sales are normally tracked using cookies (small text files set on the visitor's computer), and the duration of how long to keep them on the visitor's machine is called the cookie life. In our context, it means the time period between the click on the affiliate site and the last day when you are willing to pay that affiliate a percentage of the sale made by "their" visitor. Cookie life may be set for 30, 60, 90 or more days. Once the cookie life expires, the visitor sent by the affiliate becomes "your" visitor. If, for example, the cookie life is set at 60 days, and someone (whom an affiliate referred) makes a purchase from you three months down the road, the affiliate is not paid the commission.

Q.: What about those visitors that have their cookies turned off?

A.: I want to address this question, because it is one that you may be asked by your affiliates. Yes, it is true that some people disable cookies in their browsers, believing it provides them with higher online security through privacy. However, cookies are now such an essential part of the day-to-day

Internet use that many websites will simply not function properly for the end-user unless he/she has the cookies enabled. Most merchant's shopping carts won't work if the user's cookies are disabled. Cookies also help create a more positive and enjoyable Internet experience through customization of each individual user's utilization of the Internet.

The main question should be: how many online users actually turn cookies off? Commission Junction quotes 1%. Many online advertising agencies, affiliate networks, and websites stress the harmlessness of cookies and educate the end-users to keep those cookies turned on. For example, AllAboutCookies.org, a website of the Interactive Advertising Bureau Europe, emphasizes:

> "Because cookies are just harmless files, or keys, they cannot look into your computer and find out information about you, your family, or read any material kept on your hard-drive. Cookies simply unlock a computer's memory and allow a website to recognize users when they return to a site by opening doors to different content or services. It is technically impossible for cookies to read personal information."

Let us return back to the statistics, as they are what is most relevant to the problem in question. In an article on "Internet privacy", Wikipedia states: "Many users choose to disable cookies in their web browsers". However, it does not give any statistics to how many users! Commission Junctions states that the number is only 1%, Opentracker.net quotes 3%. Regardless of how hard I tried, I was unable to find any other statistics on the issue. If one looks at the overall statistics of Internet users – according to Nielsen//NetRatings' researches, in the USA alone 200,000,000+ people use Internet – 1%-3% is "many users". It is basically anywhere between two and six million people in the United States alone. However, it is by far *not* a considerable number, as 97%-99% of users have those cookies turned on. Moreover, we do not know how many of those that disable cookies in their browsers are online shoppers. Not all Internet users shop online. Considering that only about 75%-80% of Americans shop online, it is safe to assume that some of those that disable cookies in their browsers may not be online shoppers at all.

Conclusion: Unless you are using an affiliate tracking that is not dependent on cookies, the affiliate program will not be able to credit affiliate accounts on the sales made by those users that have disabled their cookies. However, the percentage of users that disable cookies is small enough for your affiliates not to give it too much concern.

Q.: If two affiliates send me the same visitor, do both get the commission?

A.: No, only the last affiliate that sent you the visitor who turned into a customer gets the commission. This is provided by the fact that the cookie set on the visitor's computer at his first click on an affiliate link is overwritten by a new cookie when he/she clicks on another affiliate's link.

Q.: What if a customer returns the product?

A.: If a customer returns the product they ordered through an affiliate link (be it their whole order, or a part of it), you are not liable to pay your affiliate a commission on that product or that full order (depending on what was returned). In the very beginning of this chapter we mentioned that "most merchants tie the compensation of affiliates solely to the registered and *confirmed* sales". You may void an affiliate transaction if any of the following behaviors are registered:

Customer Behavior
- Payment authorization failed
- Fraudulent sale
- Returned order or unclaimed shipment
- Duplicate order
- Cancelled order

Affiliate Behavior
- Fraudulent transaction
- Test transaction
- Self-referral (if you do not allow it)

Merchant Behavior/Circumstances
- Test transaction*
- Order non-fulfillment

The list may be longer, depending on your affiliate program agreement/restrictions, but the above list covers the most popular reasons for reversals. Beware that an affiliate may request you to provide proof of the above. Do not leave such affiliate requests unattended, as this will undermine their trust in you and the transparency of your affiliate program. *Also, when you place a test transaction at your website, and you do not want to test a particular affiliate link, make sure you have cleared your cookies before placing the order through. Otherwise, a commission may be credited to the affiliate account whose website you have visited last.

A word of warning to close with: do not abuse your right to void sales. Some online industries – hosting, for example – are sadly known for a large volume of reversed affiliate transactions. Excessive numbers of such reversals can create suspicion on the part of the merchant, thus compromising the issue of trust, a cornerstone of any merchant-affiliate relation.

2
Launch Phase

Q.: What should the base commission rate be?

A.: When deciding at what level to set the default commission rate, calculate what you can afford to pay and remember to leave room for time-limited commission increase offers, promos, and private offers.

There are various opinions on how to calculate what you can afford to pay your affiliates. Some would say to pay as much of your gross profit margin as possible, and if you can afford to pay out as much as 50% of that margin – do so. The idea behind such thinking is to be generous to your affiliates, as you indeed *should* be. However, do not forget to think three steps ahead, and leave a little room for growth. Starting from around 20-25% of your gross profit margin may be a better idea to determine the maximum affiliate commission you want to pay.

If your calculations show that the maximum you can afford to pay your affiliates is 15% of each sale that they send to you, do *not* set the base commission at the 15%. Leave the largest possible commission for private offers. Private offers are essentially special commission rates offered to a limited number of affiliates – those that already have the traffic you are interested in (or already promoting your direct competitors), and hence, are able to send you a considerable amount of traffic and sales. Again, let me stress that you want to leave the maximum possible commission amount for those private offers.

I have also mentioned time-limited commission increases and promotions. If you are going to be managing your affiliate program the very best way you can, you will be running various promotions (the third part of this book will help you with those), and you will, at times, need some room to raise that commission level or to offer various bonuses. I advise my clients to set the default commission rate at least 20% lower than the maximum commission they are willing to pay out. Some super affiliates, however, will not consider a 20% increase to be substantial, and will only consider 50% or even 100% commission increases. I manage one program that has their base commission set at 10%, but pays one of its affiliates 15% and another 18%.

Q.: What about the second tier commission?

A.: By all means, avoid multi-tier commission structures. Unless you are starting your affiliate program to recruit affiliate program directories to find affiliates for you, do not even start thinking about that second tier. Put yourself in the affiliate's shoes. What would you yourself rather do: recruit competitors (other affiliates) to earn the first tier money, while you get your second tier cuts, or would you rather get a larger first (and only) tier commission from the start?

I have conducted a poll among affiliates. The question of the poll was: "2nd Tier Program – Will You Join or Not?": 0% voted for "Absolutely!", 6.25% for "I'll join it, and promote both the 1st and the 2nd tier", and 93.75% cast their votes for "No, but I would rather get a higher commission, as I won't be promoting the 2nd tier". The results of the poll speak louder than any words.

Q.: May I lower the commission rate at a later time?

A.: I am not asked this question very often. Perhaps because I tend to include the answer to it in the above question (that regarding the default commission), foreseeing the possibility of a dreadful mistake. Yes, lowering the commission rate at any time during the life of your affiliate program would indeed be a grave mistake. To be frank, it would more than likely bury your affiliate program. Put yourself into your affiliate's place and you will understand why. Respect your affiliates, and let your actions mirror this respect.

Q.: At what level should the cookies life be set?

A.: There are pros and cons to setting the cookies life at longer periods. The major advantage is certainly the fact that lifetime cookies or 365 days cookies – whatever your network or in-house software supports – are extremely pleasing to the affiliate's eye. Statistics also speaks in favor of the lifetime cookies. Anywhere between 20% and 35% of online users delete cookies on a regular basis (weekly or monthly), either manually or with the help of various anti-spyware applications.

However, there are also other statistics that are relevant to the issue in question. My analysis of return days in which sales occurred across the programs that I manage showed the following:

same day sale	75%
sale within 1-30 days since the first visit	19.5%
sale within 31-60 days	3%
sale within 61-90 days	2%
sale over 91 days after the first visit	0.5%

In light of the above statistics, the optimum cookie life for a merchant is anywhere between 60 and 90 days. I have a merchant whose cookies life we had set at 60 days, but on a daily basis I offer affiliates cookies increases to 180 and 365 days for their activity. Just as I advise on the commission rate, leave a little room for increases with cookies, as well.

Q.: What is most important to an affiliate?

A.: In the course of the past 6 months I have seen numerous polls and questionnaires on this subject, and most affiliates agree that *conversion ratio* and *commission rate* are the two most important factors they look at prior to joining an affiliate program. Affiliate networks display both of these metrics publicly, and when an affiliate looks for a hosting

33

affiliate program, he/she will look through the list of all hosting programs available on the network, choosing the one that offers the best combination of these two factors. Among other decision-influencing factors, affiliates mention the following:

- Average order size
- Cookies life (the longer – the better)
- EPC (which can be calculated as the *average order size* multiplied by the *conversion ratio* multiplied by the *commission rate*)
- Good datafeed (well-structured & frequently updated)
- Parasite-free program/network
- Quality navigation & design of the merchant's website, as well as an easy ordering process
- Recognizability & reputation of the affiliate manager in charge of the program
- Recognizability of the merchant's brand & merchant's overall reputation
- Reliable payment
- Reliable tracking
- Reversal rate
- Suitability for the niches an affiliate works in
- Width of demographical coverage by the merchant's unique value proposition & suitability of the merchant's product(s) for large number of Internet shoppers

The list could go on – and we will somewhat return to it in a different form in the "What to stay away from?" question below – but the majority of affiliates agree that what ultimately matters most is the amount of the check they get from the merchant. All of the above, as well as many other factors, are therefore looked at through the prism of the final remuneration for the time spent on the promotion of the program.

Q.: How important is it to have a Program Agreement for affiliates?

A.: An agreement that clearly outlines the "do's and don'ts", as well as the responsibilities and obligations of both parties, will save you a lot of headache in the future. I would highly recommend coming up with a program agreement that is as comprehensive and as all-encompassing as possible right from the start. Spelling things out from the onset will demonstrate to your prospective affiliates that you are serious about the business. By definition, an affiliate program is a contractual agreement between an affiliate and a merchant. It is amazing how many programs operate without program agreements in place. Having taken a list of 100 affiliate programs from the same vertical, I conducted a study on the existence and quality of affiliate program descriptions. The study was conducted in December 2006, and here are the results it revealed:

	PRODUCE SALES	30 DAY EPC UNDER $.50
No agreement	24%	27%
Short agreement	18%	18%
Full agreement	7%	6%

Once the above research was completed, two points struck me: (1) 51% of merchants had no program agreements whatsoever, and (2) statistics for converting and non or poorly-converting merchants were basically the same: 24-27%, 18% and 6-7%. The latter fact proves that there is a tendency towards no agreement. The former may lead some to improper conclusions. Before such statistics as "24% of *converting* merchants have no agreements" misleads you into thinking that you can have no program agreement and still do well (or even very well), let me give you an example. I had a client that ran an affiliate program with a detailed program agreement, yet had some important points missing from it. One of these missing points was the trademark bidding restrictions clause for those affiliates that use pay-per-click campaigns as the foundation of their affiliate marketing. Analysis showed that this particular merchant ended up paying over 50% of his commissions to an affiliate that was basically a trademark violator. This affiliate would not only bid on the merchant's names, but outbid the merchant himself, taking away a good part of his business – that part that was based on the name trademarked by the merchant. When a company spends millions of advertising dollars on Super Bowl commercials that last seconds, it does so to build its brand. Each brand should be protected in every marketing agreement, and the affiliate program agreement is no exception. My main point is: do not misinterpret the above-quoted statistics for well-converting merchants. Chances are that those who convert well without having an affiliate program agreement are paying twice.

Let us now turn to another group of merchants – those with short agreements. A deeper analysis of their agreements revealed an interesting fact: over four fifths of merchants in the "short agreements" group seemed to confuse the predestination of the program agreement with the purpose of the program's description. The confusion exists between the producing programs and the non-producing ones, alike. Short texts (many as short as one line!) based on phrases such as: "we only agree to pay commissions on confirmed orders", "we are committed to satisfying our customers 100%", "our product will make people trust you", "we have a 30-day money back guarantee", "we are the developers of the first product of this kind", "we are featured on NBC, ABC, etc", "we are offering 12% per sale", and "our conversion rates exceeded those of our competitors", abound in the program agreement's place. Merchants that have such "program agreements" clearly miss the "agreement" component of the phrase. Both online stores running affiliate programs, as well as affiliate managers who manage them, should remember that terms like "Affiliate Program Agreement" and "Terms of Service" (TOS) are used in affiliate marketing interchangeably. In any business, Terms of Service outline the terms and conditions, the rules and regulations by which one must agree to abide by in order to use a service. The affiliate marketing industry is no exception. The above-quoted basic definition of the TOS is to be kept in mind as one works on an affiliate program's agreement.

Among the "short agreements" I came across the following, which I have paraphrased: "As other affiliate programs, we do provide you with the regulations for our affiliate program, but those are similar or within terms and conditions that the affiliate network has in place." This is okay, but what about your PPC policy, or policy regarding affiliates purchasing through their own links? Aspects such as these are never described in affiliate network's agreements, as they are too merchant-specific, and may differ from one affiliate program to another.

Another interesting fact: close to 70% of those that have "full agreements" have obviously copied them – often word-for-word – from their competitor's affiliate agreements.

To give you some good starting guidance on what an affiliate program agreement should look like, I am hereby including an agreement I had put together for the very first program I managed, and continue to manage: the RussianLegacy.com's affiliate program. Feel free to use it, but please take your time to modify it to suit your own situation:

FOREWORD

Our affiliates are very important to us. We do our best to treat you with the fairness and respect you deserve. We simply ask the same consideration of you. We have written the following affiliate agreement with you in mind, as well as to protect our company's good name. So please bear with us as we take you through this legal formality.

If you have any questions, please don't hesitate to let us know. We are strong believers in straight-forward and honest communication. For quickest results please email us at affiliate_program@russianlegacy.com. You can also reach us via phone, toll-free: 1-877-787-7467 (7am-3pm Eastern Standard Time).

Best regards,

Evgenii "Geno" Prussakov
RussianLegacy.com Affiliate Manager

AFFILIATE AGREEMENT

PLEASE READ THE ENTIRE AGREEMENT.

YOU MAY PRINT THIS PAGE FOR YOUR RECORDS.

THIS IS A LEGAL AGREEMENT BETWEEN YOU AND RUSSIAN LEGACY, INC. (DBA RUSSIANLEGACY.COM)

BY SUBMITTING THE ONLINE APPLICATION YOU ARE AGREEING THAT YOU HAVE READ AND UNDERSTAND THE TERMS AND CONDITIONS OF THIS AGREEMENT AND THAT YOU AGREE TO BE LEGALLY RESPONSIBLE FOR EACH AND EVERY TERM AND CONDITION.

1. Overview

This Agreement contains the complete terms and conditions that apply to you becoming an affiliate in RussianLegacy.com's Affiliate Program. The purpose of this Agreement is to allow HTML linking between your web site and the RussianLegacy.com web site. Please note that throughout this Agreement, "we," "us," and "our" refer to RussianLegacy.com, and "you," "your," and "yours" refer to the affiliate.

2. Affiliate Obligations

2.1. To begin the enrollment process, you will complete and submit the online application at the ShareASale.com server. The fact that we auto-approve applications does not imply that we may not re-evaluate your application at a later time. We may reject your application at our sole discretion. We may cancel your application if we determine that your site is unsuitable for our Program, including if it:

2.1.1. Promotes sexually explicit materials

2.1.2. Promotes violence

2.1.3. Promotes discrimination based on race, sex, religion, nationality, disability, sexual orientation, or age

2.1.4. Promotes illegal activities

2.1.5. Incorporates any materials which infringe or assist others to infringe on any copyright, trademark or other intellectual property rights or to violate the law

2.1.6. Includes "RussianLegacy.com" or variations or misspellings thereof in its domain name

2.1.7. Is otherwise in any way unlawful, harmful, threatening, defamatory, obscene, harassing, or racially, ethnically or otherwise objectionable to us in our sole discretion.

2.1.8. Contains software downloads that potentially enable diversions of commission from other affiliates in our program.

2.1.9. You may not create or design your website or any other website that you operate, explicitly or implied in a manner which resembles our website nor design your website in a manner which leads customers to believe you are RussianLegacy.com or any other affiliated business.

2.2. As a member of RussianLegacy.com's Affiliate Program, you will have access to Affiliate Account Manager. Here you will be able to review our Program's details and previously-published affiliate newsletters, download HTML code (that provides for links to web pages within the RussianLegacy.com web site) and banner creatives, browse and get tracking codes for our coupons and deals. In order for us to accurately keep track of all guest visits from your site to ours, you must use the HTML code that we provide for each banner, text link, or other affiliate link we provide you with.

2.3. RussianLegacy.com reserves the right, at any time, to review your placement and approve the use of Your Links and require that you change the placement or use to comply with the guidelines provided to you.

2.4. The maintenance and the updating of your site will be your responsibility. We may monitor your site as we feel necessary to make sure that it is up-to-date and to notify you of any changes that we feel should enhance your performance.

2.5. It is entirely your responsibility to follow all applicable intellectual property and other laws that pertain to your site. You must have express permission to use any person's copyrighted material, whether it be a writing, an image, or any other copyrightable work. We will not be responsible (and you will be solely responsible) if you use another person's copyrighted material or other intellectual property in violation of the law or any third party rights.

3. RussianLegacy.com Rights and Obligations

3.1. We have the right to monitor your site at any time to determine if you are following the terms and conditions of this Agreement. We may notify you of any changes to your site that we feel should be made, or to make sure that your links to our web site are appropriate and to notify further you of any changes that we feel should be made. If you do not make the changes to your site that we feel are necessary, we reserve the right to terminate your participation in the RussianLegacy.com Affiliate Program.

3.2. RussianLegacy.com reserves the right to terminate this Agreement and your participation in the RussianLegacy.com Affiliate Program immediately and without notice to you should you commit fraud in your use of the RussianLegacy.com Affiliate Program or should you abuse this program in any way. If such fraud or abuse is detected, RussianLegacy.com shall not be liable to you for any commissions for such fraudulent sales.

3.3. This Agreement will begin upon our acceptance of your Affiliate application, and will continue unless terminated hereunder.

4. Termination

Either you or we may end this Agreement AT ANY TIME, with or without cause, by giving the other party written notice. Written notice can be in the form of mail, email or fax. In addition, this Agreement will terminate immediately upon any breach of this Agreement by you.

5. Modification

We may modify any of the terms and conditions in this Agreement at any time at our sole discretion. In such event, you will be notified by email. Modifications may include, but are not limited to, changes in the payment procedures and RussianLegacy.com's Affiliate Program rules. If any modification is unacceptable to you, your only option is to end this Agreement. Your continued participation in RussianLegacy.com's Affiliate Program following the posting of the change notice or new Agreement on our site will indicate your agreement to the changes.

6. Payment

RussianLegacy.com uses a third party to handle all of the tracking and payment. The third party is the ShareASale.com affiliate network. Kindly review the network's payment terms and conditions..

7. Access to Affiliate Account Manager

You will create a password so that you may enter ShareASale's secure Affiliate Account Manager. From their site you will be able to receive your reports that will describe our calculation of the commissions due to you.

8. Promotion Restrictions

8.1. You are free to promote your own web sites, but naturally any promotion that mentions RussianLegacy.com could be perceived by the public or the press as a joint effort. You should know that certain forms of advertising are always prohibited by RussianLegacy.com. For example, advertising commonly referred to as "spamming" is unacceptable to us and could cause damage to our name. Other generally prohibited forms of advertising include the use of unsolicited commercial email (UCE), postings to non-commercial newsgroups and cross-posting to multiple newsgroups at once. In addition, you may not advertise in any way that effectively conceals or misrepresents your identity, your domain name, or your return email address. You may use mailings to customers to promote RussianLegacy.com so long as the recipient is already a customer or subscriber of your services or web site, and recipients have the option to remove themselves from future mailings. Also, you may post to newsgroups to promote RussianLegacy.com so long as the news group specifically welcomes commercial messages. At all times, you must clearly represent yourself and your web sites as independent from RussianLegacy.com. If it comes to our attention that you are spamming, we will consider that cause for immediate termination of this Agreement and your participation in the RussianLegacy.com Affiliate Program. Any pending balances owed to you will not be paid if your account is terminated due to such unacceptable advertising or solicitation.

8.2. Affiliates that among other keywords or exclusively bid in their Pay-Per-Click campaigns on keywords such as RussianLegacy.com, Russian Legacy, RussianLegacy and/or any misspellings or similar alterations of these – be it separately or in combination with other keywords – and do not direct the traffic from such campaigns to their own website prior to re-directing it to ours, will be considered trademark violators, and their commission level will be lowered to 3% on all sales. The commission level will be changed without prior notice on the first occurrence of such PPC bidding behavior. *Important exception*: trademark violators will not get a commission reduction if their PPC ad does not suppress our own.

8.3. Affiliates are not prohibited from purchasing our products through their own affiliate links. However, such purchases will not qualify for any promos or bonuses run by our Affiliate Program.

8.4. Affiliate shall not transmit any so-called "interstitials," "Parasiteware™," "Parasitic Marketing," "Shopping Assistance Application," "Toolbar Installations and/or Add-ons," "Shopping Wallets" or "deceptive pop-ups and/or pop-unders" to consumers from the time the consumer clicks on a qualifying link until such time as the consumer has fully exited RussianLegacy's site (i.e., no page from our site or any RussianLegacy.com's content or branding is visible on the end-user's screen). As used herein a. "Parasiteware™" and "Parasitic Marketing" shall mean an application that (a) through accidental or direct intent causes the overwriting of affiliate and non affiliate commission tracking cookies through any other means than a customer initiated click on a qualifying link on a web page or email; (b) intercepts searches to redirect traffic through an installed software, thereby causing, pop ups, commission tracking cookies to be put in place or other commission tracking cookies to be overwritten where a user would under normal circumstances have arrived at the same destination through the results given by the search (search engines being, but not limited to, Google, MSN, Yahoo, Overture, AltaVista, Hotbot and similar search or directory engines); (c) set commission tracking cookies through loading of Merchant site in IFrames, hidden links and automatic pop ups that open RussianLegacy.com's site; (d) targets text on web sites, other than those web sites 100% owned by the application owner, for the purpose of contextual marketing; (e) removes, replaces or blocks the visibility of Affiliate banners with any other banners, other than those that are on web sites 100% owned by the owner of the application.

9. Grant of Licenses

9.1. We grant to you a non-exclusive, non-transferable, revocable right to (i) access our site through HTML links solely in accordance with the terms of this Agreement and (ii) solely in connection with such links, to use our logos, trade names, trademarks, and similar identifying material (collectively, the "Licensed Materials") that we provide to you or authorize for such purpose. You are only entitled to use the Licensed

Materials to the extent that you are a member in good standing of RussianLegacy.com's Affiliate Program. You agree that all uses of the Licensed Materials will be on behalf of RussianLegacy.com and the good will associated therewith will inure to the sole benefit of RussianLegacy.com.

9.2. Each party agrees not to use the other's proprietary materials in any manner that is disparaging, misleading, obscene or that otherwise portrays the party in a negative light. Each party reserves all of its respective rights in the proprietary materials covered by this license. Other than the license granted in this Agreement, each party retains all right, title, and interest to its respective rights and no right, title, or interest is transferred to the other.

10. Disclaimer

RUSSIANLEGACY.COM MAKES NO EXPRESS OR IMPLIED REPRESENTATIONS OR WARRANTIES REGARDING RUSSIANLEGACY.COM SERVICE AND WEB SITE OR THE PRODUCTS OR SERVICES PROVIDED THEREIN, ANY IMPLIED WARRANTIES OF RUSSIANLEGACY.COM ABILITY, FITNESS FOR A PARTICULAR PURPOSE, AND NON-INFRINGEMENT ARE EXPRESSLY DISCLAIMED AND EXCLUDED. IN ADDITION, WE MAKE NO REPRESENTATION THAT THE OPERATION OF OUR SITE WILL BE UNINTERRUPTED OR ERROR FREE, AND WE WILL NOT BE LIABLE FOR THE CONSEQUENCES OF ANY INTERRUPTIONS OR ERRORS.

11. Representations and Warranties

You represent and warrant that:

11.1. This Agreement has been duly and validly executed and delivered by you and constitutes your legal, valid, and binding obligation, enforceable against you in accordance with its terms;

11.2. You have the full right, power, and authority to enter into and be bound by the terms and conditions of this Agreement and to perform your obligations under this Agreement, without the approval or consent of any other party;

11.3. You have sufficient right, title, and interest in and to the rights granted to us in this Agreement.

12. Limitations of Liability

WE WILL NOT BE LIABLE TO YOU WITH RESPECT TO ANY SUBJECT MATTER OF THIS AGREEMENT UNDER ANY CONTRACT, NEGLIGENCE, TORT, STRICT LIABILITY OR OTHER LEGAL OR EQUITABLE THEORY FOR ANY INDIRECT, INCIDENTAL, CONSEQUENTIAL, SPECIAL OR EXEMPLARY DAMAGES (INCLUDING, WITHOUT LIMITATION, LOSS OF REVENUE OR GOODWILL OR ANTICIPATED PROFITS OR LOST BUSINESS), EVEN IF WE HAVE BEEN ADVISED OF THE POSSIBILITY OF SUCH DAMAGES. FURTHER, NOTWITHSTANDING ANYTHING TO THE CONTRARY CONTAINED IN THIS AGREEMENT, IN NO EVENT SHALL RUSSIANLEGACY.COM'S CUMULATIVE LIABILITY TO YOU ARISING OUT OF OR RELATED TO THIS AGREEMENT, WHETHER BASED IN CONTRACT, NEGLIGENCE, STRICT LIABILITY, TORT OR OTHER LEGAL OR EQUITABLE THEORY, EXCEED THE TOTAL COMMISSION FEES PAID TO YOU UNDER THIS AGREEMENT.

13. Indemnification

You hereby agree to indemnify and hold harmless RussianLegacy.com, and its subsidiaries and affiliates, and their directors, officers, employees, agents, shareholders, partners, members, and other owners, against any and all claims, actions, demands, liabilities, losses, damages, judgments, settlements, costs, and expenses (including reasonable attorneys' fees) (any or all of the foregoing hereinafter referred to as "Losses") insofar as such Losses (or actions in respect thereof) arise out of or are based on (i) any claim that our use of the affiliate trademarks infringes on any trademark, trade name, service mark, copyright, license, intellectual property, or other proprietary right of any third party, (ii) any misrepresentation of a representation or warranty or breach of a covenant and agreement made by you herein, or (iii) any claim related to your site, including, without limitation, content therein not attributable to us.

14. Confidentiality

All confidential information, including, but not limited to, any business, technical, financial, and customer information, disclosed by one party to the other during negotiation or the effective term of this Agreement which is marked "Confidential," will remain the sole property of the disclosing party, and each party will keep in confidence and not use or disclose such proprietary information of the other party without express written permission of the disclosing party.

15. Miscellaneous

15.1. You agree that you are an independent contractor, and nothing in this Agreement will create any partnership, joint venture, agency, franchise, sales representative, or employment relationship between you and RussianLegacy.com. You will have no authority to make or accept any offers or representations on our behalf. You will not make any statement, whether on Your Site or any other of Your Site or otherwise, that reasonably would contradict anything in this Section.

15.2. Neither party may assign its rights or obligations under this Agreement to any party, except to a party who obtains all or substantially all of the business or assets of a third party.

15.3. This Agreement shall be governed by and interpreted in accordance with the laws of the State of Delaware without regard to the conflicts of laws and principles thereof.

15.4. You may not amend or waive any provision of this Agreement unless in writing and signed by both parties.

15.5. This Agreement represents the entire agreement between us and you, and shall supersede all prior agreements and communications of the parties, oral or written.

15.6. The headings and titles contained in this Agreement are included for convenience only, and shall not limit or otherwise affect the terms of this Agreement.

15.7. If any provision of this Agreement is held to be invalid or unenforceable, that provision shall be eliminated or limited to the minimum extent necessary such that the intent of the parties is effectuated, and the remainder of this agreement shall have full force and effect.

Despite its length, I want to stress that the above is still quite a general agreement. There is plenty of room to make it more business-specific, which I highly encourage you to do as you put together an agreement of your own.

Q.: What are affiliate datafeeds?

A.: Any datafeed is essentially a file (.CSV, .XML, .XLS or any other type) that lists all your product information, such as product ID, product name, description, price, stock availability, etc. The format of the affiliate datafeed is normally such that the affiliate can interpret and understand it, be it with or without the help of any additional piece of software. By supplying affiliates with datafeeds, merchants are aiming at enabling them to feature their products right at the affiliate websites. For this purpose, besides the above-quoted pieces of information, they also include URL paths to thumbnail and larger product images, URL's leading to the pages where the individual products are featured, product categorization, and often, even product-specific keywords. Affiliates may import merchant datafeeds into their websites with the help of such software applications as WebMerge, online-based solutions such as PopShops, GoldenCAN and Datafeedr.com, or by possessing relevant programming skills themselves. The final goal is to present the whole merchant's product line on the affiliate website, giving the visitors of the latter a chance to browse, search, and view the products right on the website itself. The customer is transferred to the merchant website only once he/she clicks a "Buy", "More Info", "Purchase" or any other similar button on the affiliate website. Therefore, merchant datafeeds have a powerful potential to enhance most any affiliate website.

Once an affiliate program is started, you will have a chance to review the affiliate datafeed specifications that your network (or in-house software) expects you to go by.

Q.: What is more important: banners/links, coupons or datafeeds?

A.: First of all, this question is akin to asking which affiliates are more important: those that use banners/links, datafeeds, or coupons? It is really an improper way to look at things. Let me just say that all are important, and your aim is to provide all of these affiliate groups with data, graphics and links with which to work.

Secondly, let's look at the statistics. In November 2006, I ran polls at several affiliate message boards, asking affiliates to let me know what converts best for them: banners/links, coupons, or datafeeds. The results of the polls looked like this (I am now quoting the results received across various affiliate communities): 45% voted for banners/links, 12.6% for coupons, 28.8% for datafeeds, and 13.6% voted for "other". All of these deserve your closest attention. Make sure your affiliate program duly supports all of these types of affiliates.

Those that voted for "other" were asked to specify their choice. They mentioned such linking options as images with logos, keywords, specific niche product picture links, dynamic links, email templates, bestsellers, search forms, and interactive banners.

Q.: What are text links?

A.: Text links are a kind of hyperlink. In opposition to image or script-based hyperlinks, text links have only text in the "body" of the link. Many affiliates use them, positioning them within the content that is of an immediate use to the website visitor.

Q.: How effective are text links?

A.: Returning back to the results of the polls quoted above, out of the 45% of affiliates that voted for banners/links, over four-fifths said that text links convert best for them. This is an extremely important piece of information. Use it while managing your affiliate program. Provide your affiliates with a substantial array of text links leading to as many specific sections of your website as possible.

Q.: What text links work best?

A.: The answer is simple: those that are narrowly *deep-linked*. Nielsen Norman Group's studies of e-commerce usability show that getting from the homepage of the website to the correct product page accounts for over a quarter of all failures. NNG also measured that improved linking – and by extension, enhanced e-commerce site's usability – can double an online merchant's sales! It is obvious why generic affiliate links seldomly convert as successfully as the deep links. Website's homepage is just one of the ways to enter the website, and its content may sometimes not fit the individual needs of any given affiliate. Deep-link, deep-link, and deep-link again. Treat deep-linking as one of your main responsibilities. Remember two things: (i) text links convert 8+ times better than banner links, and (ii) deeply-linked text links convert 2 times better than those that are generic.

The phrase "text link" consists of two semantic components: "text" and "link". Affiliates may always improve the quality of the first one (the "text"), but they may not always be able to improve the quality of the second (the "link"). Provide them with as vast a selection of a deeply-linked text links as possible, covering as much ground as possible. If you have a website with a total of 10 sections and 49 sub-sections, you should have *at least* 70 text links: one for each section, one for each sub-section, one for the homepage, and ten for each of your bestsellers (leading to specific product pages). Also, whenever possible, do provide your affiliates with a way/tool to build their own deep links.

Q.: What size banners do you recommend having?

A.: The banner size (and quantity, I should add) issue is an extremely important one. You can not understate it by saying that an affiliate manager/merchant should be ready to put together as many banners as affiliates they recruit. Yes, there is a concrete set of banner sizes that I would recommend every affiliate program to have. However, you have to be prepared that affiliates will ask you for banners of custom sizes, and you want to be ready to accommodate their requests. That is the reason why I would recommend merchants recognize the fact that graphic design skills are definitely an advantage when they are looking for an affiliate manager.

Below are the sizes you would want to eventually have for your program (arranging them in the order of importance and affiliate demand):

88x31 pixels button - 3-5 banners
468x60 pixels - 3-5
125x125 pixels - 3-5
120x60 pixels - 3-5

160x300 pixels - 3-5
120x240 pixels - 2-3
120x600 pixels - 2-3
234x60 pixels - 2-3
254x331 pixels - 2-3
728x90 pixels - 1-2
720x300 pixels - 1-2
300x250 pixels - 1-2

Do not underestimate the importance of well-designed 88x31 pixels buttons. Many affiliates love them because they can fit them in just about any place on their websites. They do convert, and they are also excellent for creating lists of merchants. However, many affiliate managers are ignoring these little pieces of creative. They may deem it hard to create a nice aggressive banner of that size, and for this reason they may simply skip it. Your affiliates will not appreciate this. Please let *them* decide what will fit their websites and what won't. Yes, you are there to advise and guide, but not offering that little button (or preferably, a few buttons) in the selection of your creative, or not agreeing to create one when they specifically ask you, will not build your affiliate program a good affiliate support reputation.

Another point to be made pertains to monitoring the tendencies and statistics in the graphical ads sphere throughout the Internet. Such statistics are not only viable for the company's overall advertising campaigns, but can also be powerfully utilized in putting up affiliate creatives that will enhance your program, putting you one step ahead of your competitors in the affiliate support arena. A September-October 2006 Nielsen//NetRatings report on the most popular ad sizes revealed the following breakdown of the popularity index between different banners: leaderboard (728x90) – 25%, medium rectangle 300x250 – 18%, wide skyscraper (160x600) – 14%, full banner (468x60) – 8%, non-standard dimension banners – 8%, skyscraper (120x600) – 7%, rectangle (180x150), square button (125x125), large rectangle (336x280) and button #1 (120x90) – 3% each, and 9% share of other sizes. Some of these banner sizes are not the most traditional creative sizes, but do ask your affiliates if they could be of use to them, anyway. They will appreciate your care in asking and will recognize your willingness to go out of your way for them.

Q.: Are there any specific guidelines for affiliate banner creation?

A.: Definitely. These would be:

- No banner should have your URL spelled out on it. Affiliates do not like it, as it leaves the option for the end user to by-pass the click, then type in the URL into the address bar directly.
- It is preferable that each banner has a clear call to action on it (preferably animated, but not too intrusive). Do not assume that the end user realizes that your banner is on the affiliate website for him/her to click on. Less savvy users could think it merely shows the website's affiliation with you, and nothing more.
- The affiliate banners should attractively display your products and emphasize your selling points. They may contain the name of your company (without the ".com" please).
- Avoid excessive animation. Especially flee from short time intervals between frame changes in .GIF files, which makes the text on the banners too hard (if not impossible) to read.
- Realize that while some affiliates prefer animated banners, some actually *refuse* to use them. You want to provide your affiliates with both animated and static ones.

Q.: Do I have to have coupons?

A.: You do not *have* to, but I would recommend you do. Various estimates show that anywhere between 20% and 50% of all online affiliate sales come from coupon sites. Are you sure you want to miss this channel of distribution?

I have heard merchants saying: "Our deals are better than those of our competitors. Our prices are more attractive, our orders get processed faster... we are just better. Why do affiliates constantly ask us about coupons?" Because this is what some affiliates bank on: they play on the simple human psychology of trying-to-get-a-deal before they buy, and those merchants that offer their prospective customers these deals (in the form of affiliate coupons), normally win. Not every online shopper goes out to search for coupons, but those that do should be able to find them. I know some merchants would not agree with me, but coming from the same background (for over six years I ran an online business, selling thousands of collectibles online), I think that it all comes down to the question: do you want those 20%-50% of coupon sales or not?

Q.: What coupons should I have?

A.: Just as it is with banners, you will explore new options for coupons as you go, but the following selection is one that I would recommend each merchant to have:

- One or two coupons that are good from the first through the last of the *year*. It should aim at getting the customer to spend more money than an average customer would. Examples of such coupons may include: "Free Shipping on $99+ Orders", "$15 OFF Each $120+ Order". If you do not limit the use of these coupons to an either/or setup, more than likely they will be published side by side at coupon and non-coupon websites alike.

- Two or three new coupons for each *month*. They should preferably target price points different from the ones quoted above. For example, you may run such coupons as "$5 OFF $45 Order" and "$17 OFF $100 Order" during the first month of the year, "$7 OFF $60 Order" and "$20 OFF $120 Order" during the second month, and so on. If possible, create and support dynamic links (texts or banners) that always show the current monthly coupons. This will show your affiliate that you care about their time and are willing to provide them with such a support.

- Episodically, you may choose to run *short-term* coupons. They may be valid for a time as short as a weekend, and as long as a week. To get your affiliates interested in these, you want to make them look more attractive than your regular yearly or monthly coupons. For example, you may offer a 25% discount on all orders received during a particular weekend (post-Christmas time is a good time to run something like this). Alternatively, you may choose a particular product on which your mark-up is high enough to offer something as attractive as several coupons we ran for Russian Legacy. Two of them read like this: "$200.00 OFF a Black Women's Mink Hat with Ear-Flaps" and "$300.00 OFF a Large Authentic Soviet Banner/Flag". Coupon sites are always on the look-out for such coupons.

- Run *holiday-specific* coupons; be it to reward the "early bird" purchases, or to offer more attractive deals than those of your competitors. A good example of the latter is something a gourmet food client of ours offered – free shipping with an option to choose the exact delivery date at the same time as the order placement.

- In addition to all of the above, consider running a *deal of the day* promo. It may be limited to a week, or, if your technical and time resources allow, you may run it for as long as a month or even longer. Deal of the day promos should really provide incredible bargains, and, if possible, be automatically dynamically updated on the affiliate sites. Such campaigns may have a tremendous impact on your sales.

- Finally, offer coupons *exclusive* to select affiliates, and make sure that those affiliates whom you value most are aware of your ability to do this. There will be some affiliates that will not want to put up the coupons that all other affiliates (remember, there is competition here!) are using. Exclusive coupons will get such affiliates attracted and motivated to activate their accounts by putting these coupons up at their sites.

Q.: What types of deals convert best?

A.: The more popular and better converting deals would be: dollar or percentage off coupons, free shipping deals, and discounts tied either to the number of items purchased (73% of customers go for the "Buy 2 Get 1 Free" deal offered by an ink merchant whose program we manage), or to the sale amount that qualifies the customer for a deal.

Q.: How do I put together a "killer coupon"?

A.: The following recommendations will help you put together coupons that will convert:

- Word it eloquently and attractively.
- Have a short and simple coupon code.
- Make sure the coupon is *really* offering a deal (and not something available at your website by default such as free shipping on all $70 orders, for example).
- If possible, try to offer a coupon not available through your own website or your own marketing endeavors. Coupons that are truly exclusive to affiliates are always more highly appreciated. It is okay to let your affiliates promote the same coupons you already advance on your website, but let them also have access to a set of coupons not available anywhere else but through your affiliate channel.
- Make a coupon landing page (instead of directing the traffic to your homepage).
- If possible, make a pre-coded affiliate link that would automatically apply the coupon to the shopping cart when clicked.
- Make the coupon banner available in all sizes, displaying the coupon code on each banner.
- Let your affiliates choose between a set of banners and/or a coupon code.
- Treat every holiday as a reason for a good coupon.

With time you will be getting suggestions on coupons from your affiliates. Listen to them and make use of the most valuable ideas to perfect your skill of effective coupon creation. Marketing through coupon websites should be a part of your affiliate strategy, occupying not less than 10% of your time.

Q.: Do I need to hire an affiliate manager?

A.: The answer to this question depends on two factors: (i) the size of your business, and (ii) your own capabilities. However, before we look into these, let us first define what an affiliate manager is. An *affiliate manager* is the person in charge of the management and organization of a company's affiliate program, and whose major duties include the following:

- Identifying and recruiting new affiliates
- Activating new and/or inactive affiliates
- Maintaining stimulating relationships with the current affiliates
- Developing and monitoring affiliate promotions
- Reporting for affiliate marketing promotions and activity
- Maintaining on-going communication campaigns
- Identifying and implementing other opportunities to enhance the affiliate program
- Keeping affiliates up to date on new products and any program enhancements
- Continually motivating affiliates to perform better
- Keeping track of affiliate sales and paying affiliates in a timely manner (for in-house affiliate managers)
- Monitoring and reporting on competitors' affiliate campaigns and promotions

The above outlines the fundamental and fairly generic duties and responsibilities of an affiliate manager. Such specific tasks as creating and developing an affiliate database, directing the creative development for the program, approving affiliate applications and/or pending transactions (if this is required by the program setup), developing an attractive program description, making an FAQ list for potential affiliates (to post

57

at the merchant's website), ongoing development of newsletters, participation in online affiliate forums, and many other tasks – are all included in the affiliate manager's job description and responsibilities.

Any and every affiliate program needs an affiliate manager. No business endeavor may be run by itself. Sooner or later you will want to look at optimizing the ROI in your affiliate marketing venture, and to answer this question you will either need to be thoroughly educated in affiliate program management or have access to a quality affiliate manager.

Let us return back to what we began with: (i) the size of your business, and (ii) your own capabilities. If your business is not a very large one, and/or you have plenty of time to educate yourself in affiliate program management, I would highly recommend managing the program on your own. I myself have gone the route from an online shop owner to and affiliate manager, and, later on, to an outsourced affiliate manager. The famous Russian emperor Peter the Great was known for striving to learn everything first-hand, from the inside out. Experience is an invaluable asset, especially if this experience is directly related to your particular business. If you have the capability to do so, do try the waters of affiliate program management yourself. If, however, business management is consuming a lot of your time and you have no way of taking on an additional responsibility or hiring an extra office worker, I would encourage you to look into outsourcing your affiliate program's management to an OPM. An outsourced program manager – when compared to one who is in-house – can save you much money, without compromising the quality of the program's management.

Q.: What qualifications should an AM possess?

A.: Affiliate manager is an occupation that is fairly new, and there is no exact set of qualifications typically required to work as such. You may take those below and adapt them to your own industry. The following attributes would comprise the best *basic* prerequisites for an affiliate manager:

- *College degree.* 3-4 year Bachelor's degree. The field would depend on your vertical, but marketing and advertising, business studies, business administration, e-commerce, psychology, and communications would be good general ones to favor.
- *Experience.* The absolute minimum that I would recommend considering is 2 to 4 years of work experience, out of which 1.5-2 years would be affiliate marketing experience. The longer, the better, but more experienced affiliate managers obviously tend to cost more. Also, when I say "affiliate marketing" experience, I do not imply "affiliate manager" experience only. Affiliate marketing history is full of examples of how great affiliates became tremendous affiliate managers. Please keep this in mind.
- *Knowledge.* Basic HTML, graphics applications (e.g. Photoshop), basic e-commerce operations.
- *Skills.* Excellent verbal, communication and analytical skills, attention to detail, ability to handle multiple tasks simultaneously, organizational and people management skills.
- *Character.* Self-motivated, highly initiative, enthusiastic, outgoing, flexible and responsive.

The following skills, knowledge, and abilities are not compulsory, but may be preferable for your business:

- *Skills.* Negotiating, research, copywriting.
- *Knowledge.* Foreign language(s), specific software applications, specific affiliate network knowledge, CSS, PHP, Javascript, database concepts.
- *Abilities.* Willingness to travel.

Q. What points should one pay attention to while drafting the contract?

A.: The contract implied is obviously a contract between the merchant and the affiliate manager hired to run the merchant's affiliate program. Understanding that this question and answer will be read both by merchants and affiliate managers, I have decided to make my answer as universal as possible, aiming to make it helpful to both sides of the game. It will be natural for both parties to aim at getting the most out of their contract, so reaching a sound balance between the requirements of one party and the commitments of the other will be your main goal. As in any contracting agreement, at the end of the day, both parties have to be comfortable with the conditions of the contract. If you are not comfortable with what the other party is offering you, do not be afraid to negotiate. In the years of my affiliate program management practice I have negotiated with parties that were both easy-going, as well as those that were extremely demanding. While some prefer to forego negotiation, solely trusting your word, others will require a detailed agreement. I personally am in favor of the latter, for in the long run, it helps both parties to be clear on their respective responsibilities, and it helps to determine the ultimate course the relationship will take.

OPM companies normally have a set agreement they offer their new clients to sign. Individual affiliate managers (in-house or outsourced) may not have such an agreement. I hope that the following guidelines to the affiliate program management agreement will help you in the creation of your own contract.

When I sign a contract with a merchant, I personally follow this format:

1) *Definition of Services.* In as much detail as possible, outline the duties, roles, and responsibilities of the affiliate manager that is hired by the merchant. There are a good number of them listed above – in the answer to the "Do I need to hire an affiliate manager?" question. In this part of the agreement, the merchant may also want to outline the penalty that is entitled (in form of deductions form the affiliate manager's payment) for failures to carry out any specific imperative responsibilities (weekly/monthly reporting, e-mail affiliate support, newsletter publishing, etc).

2) *Term of Agreement.* This is the time period that the agreement is signed for, as well as the agreement cancellation terms and procedures. Some OPM companies insist on a 60-day termination clause. I am supportive of the termination clause itself. However, the time period that needs to pass between the termination notice and the termination itself does not need to be that long. Neither the merchant nor the affiliate manager should want to bind themselves for such a long period.

3) *Time.* Clearly state what time you expect the affiliate manager to devote to his/her services: how many

hours per week, and what minimum number of hours per month.

4) *Place.* The physical location is either on the company's premises for in-house affiliate program management, and "a location of the affiliate manager's discretion" for outsourced AM's.

5) *Payment Terms.* These can vary widely. It is recommended not only to have a set monthly fee, but also a performance bonus. Performance bonus is specifically defined as "a percentage of all affiliate sales, and is collected in addition to the monthly fee". For the merchant, it ensures the AM is motivated to keep the program growing. For the AM, it essentially provides a "no cap" arrangement, making the job follow the standard affiliate marketing model: the more you sell – the more you're paid. I have had agreements for full 100% prepayment, 60-40 payment structure (60% in advance, 40% at the end of the month when the performance bonus is paid), and small monthly fees tied to a large performance bonus, etc. One of my more shrewd clients put together the following payment model (I am quoting the actual contract, replacing the amounts only):

For the work performed in accordance with this agreement the affiliate manager will be paid at the rate of $4,500.00 (four thousand five hundred US Dollars) per month *or* the below-outlined commission structure, whichever is greater for the first six months. After the first six months the $4,500 minimum guarantee is going to be replaced by a $1,500.00 (one thousand five hundred US Dollars) monthly management fee *plus* the below-outlined commission structure. If the commission is greater than $4,500 during the first six months, then the $1,500 monthly management fee will be added. The affiliate manager will submit an invoice, and the company will pay the affiliate manager one month in advance. The amount due is to be paid by the 10th of each month. In the event of the payment running overdue, the affiliate manager may stop all work until the payment is received. In the event of the payment running 10 business days overdue, the affiliate manager may cease the relationship, notifying the client in writing, by certified mail, e-mail with reading confirmation, or personal delivery.

Performance Bonus. The consultant will be paid a monthly "performance bonus", specifically defined as a percentage of all affiliate sales, and collected in addition to the above fee. The performance bonus rate is going to be calculated as follows:

MONTHLY SALES	COMMISSION
From $0-$10,000	**10%** commission with guaranteed minimum of **$4,500** per month for first 6 months
From $10,000-$15,000	Calculated at **15%** commission
$15,000+	Calculated at **20%** commission

The consultant should include the exact amount due in the invoice submitted.

6) *Employment Benefits.* If you are hiring an in-house worker, you will want to outline those here. If you are hiring an OPM, stress that no benefits are

provided and "the affiliate manager shall be responsible for payment of all local taxes arising out of the manager's activities in accordance with the contract".

7) *Confidential Information.* Here you should have your non-disclosure clause regarding the merchant's "trade secrets, processes, data, procedures, know-how, intellectual property, discoveries, developments, designs, improvements, inventions, techniques, marketing plans, business plans and methods of the merchant's operations, strategies, forecasts, software, software documentation, financial statements, budgets, projections, licenses, prices, costs, client and supplier lists, and information pertaining to employee training, compensation and bonuses".

8) *Conflicting Management.* It is recommended that in your agreement you have a separate clause regarding the management of the competing affiliate programs, whereby the affiliate manager commits to "not engage in any other employment, occupation, consulting or other business activity related to the business in which the merchant is now involved or becomes involved during the Term of the Agreement, nor will the affiliate manager engage in any other activities that conflict with the affiliate manager's obligations to the merchant".

9) *Non-Competition.* Some merchants also add a separate non-competition clause to their agreement with the affiliate manager, whereby the latter commits to "not either directly or indirectly engage in (whether as an employee, consultant, proprietor, partner, director) … in the financing, operation, management or control of, any person, firm,

corporation or business that produces or sells products that directly compete with any of the merchant's products".

The agreement may also contain clauses pertaining to the solicitation of employees, contact with the merchant's suppliers, affiliates that were on board the merchant's affiliate program before the management was taken over by the new affiliate manager, and other additional clauses. However, I believe that the first eight of the above-mentioned points cover most of the areas important to both parties in the contract.

Q.: How much should I pay my affiliate manager?

A.: It depends on the following: (i) the industry, (ii) the experience of the person you are hiring, and (iii) whether you are looking for an in-house affiliate manager or have decided to outsource the work. The obvious benefits of hiring an OPM include avoiding health/401k benefit expenses, office space/computer costs, and training expenses. The ostensible disadvantage is a looser accountability, but with a properly worded contract you may definitely define the types and frequency of the reports you want to get from your OPM.

Roughly one third of all affiliate managers (in-house and OPMs taken together) make under $50,000 a year, another third makes between $50,000 and $80,000, close to 15% make between $80,000 and $100,000, and around 20% make over $100,000 a year. I know several OPMs that make over $250,000 a year, but these are definitely exceptions to the rule.

In-house position paychecks generally tend to range from $50,000 to around $85,000. The exact figure largely depends on the experience, which carries with it affiliate manager's education, creativity, popularity, and the number of contacts in the industry (among other affiliate managers and affiliates

65

alike). OPM fee ranges are not as tight as those of the in-house affiliate managers'. By and large, OPM charges fluctuate between $1,000 and $10,000 per month. The lower the fee, the larger the performance bonus attached to it. Very seldomly would any OPM work on a "performance compensation only" pattern. It is erroneous to presuppose that when you are paying them a flat monthly fee they are no longer interested in performing. If you as a merchant are hesitant to pay a large monthly fee, negotiate a lower one with a larger performance compensation attached. Also, make sure you word your contract in such a way that, on mutual agreement, you could always go up to a larger monthly fee with a smaller performance bonus.

As in any business, you can always find a worker that will fit into the budget you have apportioned for the position to which he/she is hired. Two hints about paying them too little: (i) do ask for recommendations before you sign anything, and (ii) beware that a lower quality of service may be reflected in a lower level of pay.

3
Pro Level

Q.: How do I recruit affiliates?

A.: I must admit, I hesitated as to where I should include this question, as it is probably one that is asked by affiliate managers more frequently than any other. It is a great question that may be asked both on the launch, and on the pro level. I have decided to include it as the first question in the latter section, believing it to be a good inter-phase subject to examine.

So how do we go about recruiting those affiliates that are going to send us traffic and sales? One of the common misconceptions of merchants starting new affiliate programs is a belief that once they have invested into the start-up of their program, no other investments are required; that the rest will "take care of itself." I have heard merchants telling me: "We have tried affiliate marketing and it hasn't worked for us". When investigating deeper, I would find out in 95% of the cases that their "trying of affiliate marketing" consisted of starting an affiliate program and posting the information about it in several affiliate program directories throughout the Internet. To this I would say: is that it?! Are you telling me you have "tried it"? This may come as a shock, but if that's all you've done, you have not even taken a tiny bite out of it! It's no wonder why you have never seen any sales! When an affiliate program is started you have to be ready to invest. You may invest money or time, depending on which of these you, the merchant, have in greater supply. Affiliate recruitment may either be done on one's own, or someone may be hired to do the job for you.

Here are some methods for affiliate recruitment you may use:

- *Online Forums.* In Ancient Roman times "forums" were places of meetings for judicial or public business activity. Nowadays, this word is more

69

often used for online communities or "message boards," where each member is free to discuss or voice out his/her ideas, interacting with the other members of the forum. Any merchant/affiliate manager should allocate two types of forums: those for affiliates and those that are industry-specific. This can be done easily with the help of any major search engine. For example, if you are in a photographic business, selling digital cameras, and you have an affiliate program, you would want to make sure you're registered with the major online affiliate marketing forums, as well as photography forums, and, more specifically, digital photography forums. These forums offer you multiple options for affiliate recruitment, starting from affiliate program announcement and inclusion of your sign-up URL in your signature, to running your own affiliate support forums. Professional forums may also offer you some options to push your affiliate program. However, please keep in mind to abide by the forum's rules by not blatantly promoting your own affiliate program. This is a violation of the forum's regulations, and your account may be suspended for such behavior. It is always best to register with the forum and start posting information that is helpful to others, getting to know the people at the forum, and building your own reputation. A little down the line you may consider announcing your affiliate program, but only after getting the approval of the forum's administrator.

- *Finding Websites that Link to Your Competitors.* This can be an *extremely* powerful way of affiliate recruitment. The major reason is that such websites already have the traffic you are interested in, and getting them on board your affiliate program may boost your hits and sales. There are two ways to recruit such websites: (i) *manually*, and (ii) *automatically*. The first technique presupposes browsing the Internet, looking for such websites, manually picking up those that you would want to see among your affiliates, and then e-mailing each (faxing or calling is also an option) that you want to recruit. The second technique is based on using automated systems like Arelis for the same purpose. Arelis does a lot of work for you, but careful pre-screening of all websites it finds for you is a *must*, or you may be accused of spam. Pre-screen and hand-pick the websites you want to contact, and personalize your messages. To avoid being accused of spam, see what SpamCop.net says about e-mails that cannot be reported as spam:

Unsubscribing

On January 1, 2004, the CAN-SPAM Act became law in the US. (CAN-SPAM is an acronym for **C**ontrolling the **A**ssault of **N**on-**S**olicited **P**ornography **A**nd **M**arketing). CAN-SPAM requires all unsolicited commercial email contain a label of unsolicited commercial email (although it doesn't require a particular method or label), a working unsubscribe mechanism and a physical address for the sender. It also prohibits the use of forged or falsified headers and misleading or deceptive subject lines. Many legitimate senders are complying with some or all of the provisions of the CAN-SPAM act, but so are many spammers. CAN-SPAM compliance is not necessarily a reliable way to distinguish solicited from unsolicited email. Be aware that CAN-SPAM requires that an individual be removed from a list upon request.

So *if* you do decide to use something like Arelis, and to avoid being accused of spamming, make sure you have the working "unsubscribe" mechanism in place.

- *Finding Affiliate Websites.* These may be found by searching the Internet. Coupon affiliates may be easily discovered by such keywords as "coupon", "coupons", "rebates", etc. Datafeed affiliates may be found by typing in the name of any other merchant that also has an affiliate program, and so on. Compile a list of affiliate websites and categorize them both by affiliate type (see the "Is it helpful to categorize affiliates?" question and answer), and by the verticals they work in (do not propose a computer affiliate to sell lingerie!). Doing this will help make effective use of your database for affiliate recruitment.

- *Listing in Affiliate Program Directories.* I highly recommend listing your program in affiliate directories. They are the references affiliates go to when searching for affiliate programs, and they are normally very well positioned in search engines. Most of them do not charge you anything for listing a program. As for those that do charge, kindly see the next question for recommendations.

- *Using Network-Supported Advertising Options.* Some of these may be extremely efficient, others may not be. One of the most effective we have tried is the ShareASale's "Featured Program of the Week" spot. This spot is so popular that it is often fully booked 4-5 months in advance. What the network does in this case is to provide you with a premium slot on the page that each affiliate sees upon logging into his/her affiliate account. Within one week you can recruit hundreds of seriously-minded affiliates. Other networks offer other opportunities. Some (Buy.at in the UK, for example) would agree to include unusual promotional offers in the weekly network newsletter that goes out to *all* affiliates in the network. Talk to the network reps to find out more about the recruitment opportunities that they may offer you.

- *Cross-Program Promotions.* These may be suitable for related (but not competing) products. However, do not abuse your affiliate's trust. When they agree to receive your affiliate newsletter, they agree to receive the information that will help them succeed with your program, and may consider your aggressive pushing of some other affiliate program a spam. If you do it, do it gently. Also, beware that if you are on an affiliate network, such promotions may be in violation of the networks TOS. Do check them carefully beforehand.

Before you begin affiliate recruitment, I would strongly encourage you to read this book in its entirety. I would hate to have any of your recruiting efforts be fumbled if either the website that ran the affiliate program, or the program itself, had any of the "don'ts" mentioned in the second part of this book.

Q.: Is it wise to pay to announce/list my affiliate program?

A.: In some cases it may be extremely effective, in others it may not. Things always boil down to what you are going to get in return. Before you pay anyone to list your affiliate program, ask them the same questions you would ask a website if you were a merchant buying banner or any other ad space. Ask them about their traffic, the demographics of the visitors, and for references. Those who are more serious would have these listed right at their website, and you could contact the references directly. Those less reliable will not even reply to your e-mails. Do your homework and then make an educated decision. Do beware of con-artists, as they are very much present in the affiliate marketing industry. In the early days of my affiliate marketing education, I got stuck with one paid "affiliate directory" so deeply, that neither requests to unsubscribe nor chargeback filing(s) worked. I had to close the credit card account and get an entirely new credit card to fully "unsubscribe" from them.

Q.: How do I word my recruitment e-mail?

A.: You definitely want to make it attractive, yet not too lengthy and hard to follow. Below you may find a sample recruitment e-mail that you may modify and use for your own recruitment campaigns:

My name is <Your Name> and I am the affiliate manager for
<Name of Company> hosted at http://www.companyurl.com

I have visited your site and noticed that at <URL of the page where you found a competitor's link> you
link to ABC.com - a vendor that sells merchandise very similar to ours.

(The above paragraph may be modified to say that you have noticed that the affiliate promotes a specific type of product, or works with coupons that you also offer, or anything else that would fit the recruitment path you are going along).

Since it looks like you've got the traffic – yet are of no competition to us – we would like to collaborate with you and your website. We'd like to invite you to join our affiliate program and start earning
cash from a similar link to us (as your customers/visitors buy <Company's Product> from us). Here is the link to the description of our affiliate program:

http://www.urlToYourAffiliateProgram.com/Description.htm

Why would you want to partner with <Name of Company>? Our offer is quite unique and I believe would provide your visitors with significant value when compared to our competitors…

You may then want to discuss the advantages of your business, your free shipping offers and/or any other promos, your dedication to help your affiliates succeed, be it by offering them a toll free affiliate support phone number, a dedicated affiliate support forum, or anything of the like.

SPECIAL OFFER: If you join our Affiliate Program within the next 10 business days (i.e. by <Date Month Year>) and put up at least two links to us, I will increase the default XX% commission to XX% for you (for life!). Just contact me once the links are up. If at least two of our links (one has to be a banner of any size) are placed on a webpage with (and here you may either mention a Google PR, or an Alexa ranking, or anything else that you deem to be important), we will not only raise your commission level, but will PayPal you a $10.00 bonus.

NOTE: If you feel comfortable using datafeeds, we will provide you with an access to our full product datafeed (XXXX+ items) that you may import into your website and get an additional $10.00 instant bonus for it.

Let me know if you're interested; or feel free to go ahead and sign up with the affiliate program online. If you're not interested in the affiliate program or cannot join it for some reason, we would be happy to at least exchange links with you. So please do get back with me either way.

I'll be looking forward to hearing from you – and working with you – at your earliest convenience.

Best regards,

<Your Name>
<Name of Company> Affiliate Manager
<Company's Website> or <URL to Affiliate Program Page>

If there is any way you can include contest/prize information (e.g.: a free pass to some relevant conference), that would definitely improve your open rate. Also, do not forget to have that "working unsubscribe mechanism" in place and announce it in the end of your recruitment e-mail.

Q.: What should my approval/welcome e-mail look like?
A.: Just as is the case with the affiliate program agreements, many affiliate programs do not have a proper approval or "welcome to the program" e-mail. Many do not have *anything* whatsoever. My experience shows that out of all affiliates that any given program has on board, only 5%-14% send traffic and generate sales. Some affiliate programs I have seen have this number registered below 3.5%. "How

does this relate to the approval e-mails?" you may wonder. *Directly!* I am convinced that the more detailed your approval e-mail is – and the more convincing the follow-up reminder to put those links up is – the more productive the affiliates will be for a program. The approval e-mail is really the first piece of direct correspondence that the newly-converted affiliate receives from you. Make it display your care and concern for them. Simplify things for him/her. Do not assume the affiliate knows this industry inside and out. There will be hundreds joining your program, many not having the slightest clue as to what to do after they hit that "Submit Application" button. They could very well have the websites with the traffic you are looking for! Do not be afraid to spoon-feed. The more experienced affiliates will just skip the parts that are obvious to them.

Here is a list of details that affiliates generally like to see in the approval e-mail:

- Brief reminder/description of what your company sells
- Mention of what network the affiliate program is on (if it is not an indie) and what company (or affiliate manager) manages the program
- Concise resume of what your affiliate program offers
- Full contact details of the affiliate manager or the network representative in charge of the program management
- Basic instructions on how to start with the program (be it text links, banners, dynamic scripts, datafeeds, coupon and discount offers that are currently run by the merchant, or anything else you want them to promote)

I would like to show an example of a basic approval e-mail I sent out for one of my clients. It contains the main points you want to cover in yours. Feel free to modify it and use it for your own affiliate approval e-mail (if you do not have one already):

Dear <Affiliate's Name>,

Welcome to PrivateMDLabs affiliate program. Your web site has been approved and you are now ready to send sales and earn money with PrivateMDLabs.com. We offer confidential, convenient and affordable state-of-the-art lab procedures directly to the public - all complete with a physician's order. With our competitive 16% commission and a great conversion rate, we know you'll enjoy working with us. We already have a couple of cash incentives -- we call them GBs or "Geno bucks" -- ready for you, and I would like to share them with you at the very outset of our relationship. They are:

$10.00 GBs bonus (on top of your regular commission) with the second sale you send in
$60.00 GBs bonus once you've reached a total of $1500 in sales

Considering that our typical sales range from $250 to $450, it is obvious that the goal of $1500 in sales is more reachable with our program than with many other ones. Besides your regular 16% commission (which makes $240 on the batch of $1500), you will also receive a $60.00 GBs bonus, making your total earn as large as $300 on the first batch of $1500.

Just e-mail me once you've performed any of the bonus-qualifying actions, making sure you include your affiliate ID and the respective transaction ID's in your e-mail message, and I will credit your account the promised GBs.

We look forward to working with you and we are always here to assist you with any of your professional needs. You may want to print this email for your records. Your ShareASale numerical affiliate ID is: [AFFID] and, to help you start working your way towards the cash bonuses faster, I am hereby including several PrivateMDLabs' links/banners with your affiliate ID already embedded in the code under each banner. I hope you will find them of help.

Links encoded with your affiliate ID:

Text Link #1
<a href=CODE HERE</a>

Picture of 100x100 banner
<a href=CODE HERE</a>

Picture of 120x600 banner
<a href=CODE HERE</a>

Picture of 468x60 banner
<a href=CODE HERE</a>

Picture of 120x60 banner
<a href=CODE HERE</a>

Picture of 468x60 banner
<a href=CODE HERE</a>

We will also have our full product data feed available soon, of which we will notify you via our regular affiliate newsletter.

Should you have any questions regarding the PrivateMDLabs.com's Affiliate Program, please do not hesitate to contact me at info@amnavigator.com.

Sincerely yours,

Geno Prussakov
PrivateMDLabs.com Affiliate Manager
dedicated program management by AM Navigator

I am at your service via all IM-chats:
AIM: eprussakov77
ICQ: 207974431
YIM: eprussakov
Skype: eprussakov1

Try to personalize your approval e-mail as much a possible. Short-codes that are provided for such purposes by many networks and affiliate program software applications will greatly help you with this. The above-quoted example uses [FIRSTNAME] and [AFFID] as sample short-codes for the affiliate's name and user ID respectively. The word-processor's capabilities do not allow me to present the sample newsletter to you both vividly and with the possibility to view the code behind it (it is sent out as an HTML message), but the above should give you a basic idea of what I am talking about.

Q.: What about the denial e-mail?

A.: Affiliate application denials are as much a necessity as approvals, and one must have a policy with which to handle them. From the outset, I want to mention that there are pros and cons for having standardized denial e-mails. The obvious advantage is the fact that it saves you time on typing up individual e-mails. The major disadvantage, however, is the apparent impossibility to fully substantiate an *individual* denial message for *all* denied applications in the same form. The compromise may be found in having a multi-layer application approval/denial system/policy in place. Here is what I propose:

- Step 1a – Affiliate is approved; standard approval e-mail, personalized in the above-quoted manner, is sent.
- Step 1b – Affiliate website quoted on the application (or the affiliate profile, if your program is on a network) may not be approved until further investigation is conducted. A template message is sent out, requesting the applicant to clarify how

he/she is envisaging the promotion of your affiliate program on the website mentioned in the application. Give the affiliate 5-10 business days to reply.

- Step 2a – Affiliate replies, explaining what he/she has in mind for your affiliate program. Affiliate manager's decision on whether to approve or deny is then better grounded. Respective e-mail template (either approval or denial) is then sent.

- Step 2b - If no reply is received within the 5-10 business days: e-mail out a template message, explaining that the application has been denied due to the lack of response and apparent unsuitability of the quoted website to promote your affiliate program. At the end of the message, do have a sentence added where you state that you would be willing to re-consider the application with affiliate's due response.

The above-described pattern of processing affiliate applications is a very basic one. You may expand it to as many steps and sub-steps as you want. Take your time to create separate denial e-mails for separate groups of affiliates: one for banner farms, another for sites with nothing but a list of poorly navigated links to different merchants, and yet another for those that do not reply to you within those 5-10 business days, etc. In this way you will be able to make your denial e-mails both substantiated and as tailor-made as possible.

Word of Warning: Never assume that the website your prospective affiliate has mentioned on his affiliate account with a network is the only website he/she has. Also never assume that it is *the* website at which the affiliate is planning to promote your program. Many affiliates have dozens of different websites; some have hundreds, and a few even thousands. They either cannot fit all of them into their profile with the affiliate network, or do not want to waste their time doing this. That is why I am recommending that you always do that "Step 1b" before you decide to turn down an affiliate application. Be extremely careful. You may lose an excellent affiliate by automatically denying an application simply because the affiliate's profile lists a shoe shop, while you are promoting a digital video camera affiliate program.

Q.: An affiliate that has no website has applied to my program. What should I do??

A.: The above "never assume" advice applies here, too. Contact the affiliate, asking him/her how they are planning on promoting your website. It may be a mailing list, a PPC campaign, or something other than this. Yes, it is true that most serious affiliates would have at least some kind of a website. But again, do not assume they don't have one if they have not mentioned it. Talk to the affiliate to learn about their situation and circumstances.

Q.: What is the best way to contact affiliates?

A.: I personally communicate with my affiliates by all means available to humankind: face-to-face, phone, e-mail, instant messages, private messages in online forums, and even fax (to prospective affiliates, mostly). Out of all these, I would say that affiliates prefer e-mail over all other methods. As for phone calls and any other confronting methods of communication, make yourself available, but never insist on them. Leave your affiliates the option to schedule a phone call with you, or to join in on a phone conference at a particular time every week or month, but never insist on it.

Q.: How frequently should I keep in contact with my affiliates?

A.: Let your initial contact be a thoughtfully-put-together approval e-mail, and then contact them via your regular newsletters. No more than once a week should you contact them with a private offer or a set of coupons exclusive to affiliates (or just one particular affiliate), and always reply to their e-mails within 24 to 48 hours, the sooner the better. With time you will see that some affiliates have the possibility to reply to you very quickly, and do it in long, detailed messages, while others may be a part of so many affiliate programs that they are much too busy to stay in touch with you on a daily basis.

Also, remember that, as one of my favorite affiliates puts it, "affiliates and affiliate managers *do not* have the same interests in the game." You, as the affiliate manager, are interested in having as many affiliates as possible sending you sales, while any given affiliate is only interested in his/her own affiliate success. With this in mind, do not be too pushy in how you communicate with your better-performing affiliates. Respect what they do for you, and encourage them to do more (by various incentives), but do not approach them to share their recipes for success with others. They are not interested in educating their own competition, *you* are. That is why, as already mentioned above, first-hand affiliate experience is a must for any affiliate manager.

Q.: How often should I be sending out a newsletter?

A.: You should at least have regular monthly newsletters, but may also send them out weekly. It is important that your newsletters are informative and to the point. Remember that many affiliates have hundreds of different merchants. Make your newsletter both interesting and relevant. Make it stand out, and let it be applicable to the progress of their success. They will then value it and look forward to it.

Q.: What should my affiliate newsletters look like?

A.: There are many ways you can layout your affiliate newsletter. I personally try to follow this format:

1) Introduction/Welcome
2) Affiliate program & website news
3) Top-performers & contest winners for the previous month
4) Bonuses & contests for the current month
5) Ready-made links
6) Tool of the month
7) Conclusion

Below you may find two sample newsletters: one is a shorter version (skipping points 2, 3 and 6), the other, a fuller one. Both are based on the actual newsletters sent for two of the affiliate programs we manage.

NEWSLETTER #1 – Short Version

Dear <Affiliate's Name>,

On behalf of GourmetStation.com and AM Navigator we wish you a very Happy Thanksgiving! Thanksgiving is the time when families and friends come together around one table: some to give thanks to God, others to devote this time to their loved ones. Whatever your own convictions are, we have something for you to enjoy this month. We are calling you to offer your customers a beautiful four-course Thanksgiving Dinner for two! Not only are we calling on you to promote it, but we also want you to have it for yourself, as well. Here's what you need to do:

- Send in $499.99+ in sales between 10/30 and 11/20 and the dinner is yours **Free of Charge!**

The dinner comes with a *free delivery* and a possibility to set the *exact delivery date* (not something our competitors offer).

To ease your work, I am hereby including the whole selection of our Thanksgiving links and banners with your own affiliate ID already embedded in the code under each link/banner. All you need to do is cut and paste that code into your websites. I hope you will find this of help, and looking forward to your Thanksgiving sales!

Links Embedded With Your Affiliate ID:

Thanksgiving Text Link #1
<a href=CODE HERE</a>

Picture of 88x31 static Thanksgiving button
<a href=CODE HERE</a>

Picture of 88x31 animated Thanksgiving button
<a href=CODE HERE</a>

Picture of 100x100 static Thanksgiving banner
<a href=CODE HERE</a>

Picture of 100x100 animated Thanksgiving banner
<a href=CODE HERE</a>

Picture of 468x60 static Thanksgiving banner
<a href=CODE HERE</a>

Picture of 468x60 animated Thanksgiving banner
<a href=CODE HERE</a>

Picture of 120x600 static Thanksgiving banner
<a href=CODE HERE</a>

Picture of 120x600 animated Thanksgiving banner

`<a href=CODE HERE</a>`

Many more banners and text links may be found by logging into your affiliate account at ShareASale at http://www.shareasale.com/a-login.cfm and going to the "Get Links/ Banners / Referral URLs" hyperlink under the "GET LINKS" menu, where you will find all GourmetStation's text links and banners.

Remember that we are paying out the following cash bonuses:

- **$5.00** for putting up two links on your site (subject to affiliate manager approval)
- **$15.00** bonus (in addition to the above) on your very first sale with us
- **$50.00** bonus once you've reached a total of $500 in sales
- ...and, even better than that - a **$120.00** bonus once you've reached a total of $1000 in sales!

The above-quoted bonuses are *non*-exclusive of our Thanksgiving promo. Just e-mail me once you've performed any of the above-quoted actions, making sure you include the transaction ID's in your e-mail message, and I will credit your account the promised GBs. Also, do not hesitate to contact me directly with any and all questions regarding this promo and/or the entire affiliate program. I am here to help you succeed with the GourmetStation.com.

Sincerely yours,

Geno Prussakov
GourmetStation.com Affiliate Manager
dedicated program management by AM Navigator

I am at your service via all IM-chats:
AIM: eprussakov77
ICQ: 207974431
YIM: eprussakov
Skype: eprussakov1

NEWSLETTER #2 – Longer Version

Dear <Affiliate's Name>,

Thank you for being a part of the FunToCollect's affiliate program, and welcome to our October newsletter!

Program & Website News:

We are excited to announce to you that the number of items we hold in stock (oh yes, everything we ship is stocked, and ships next business day!) has increased from the 8,794 in September, to 9,039 in October. All of them are available for you to feature at your websites. You may import them into your sites either via our datafeed, access to which is granted to each affiliate *free of charge* and on first request. We not only offer the datafeed access for free, but also pay each affiliate a **$10.00** bonus for the import of our entire datafeed into each affiliate website. Please keep this in mind!

September Top-Performers & Contest Winners:

Our top five performers last month earned the following amounts of money:

1. $XXXX.XX
2. $XXXX.XX
3. $XXXX.XX
4. $ XXX.XX
5. $ XXX.XX

Upon the results of the September Promo, we have also awarded four **$20.00** September bonuses, two **15%** commission increases, and one **20%** increase in the month of September.

October Promo:

It is my pleasure to now announce to you our October promo campaign, which will include both cash bonuses and performance-based commission increases. This month we are willing to throw in some extra cash to reward our better-performing affiliates. The conditions are simple:

- Send $4000 or more in gross sales between 1 and 31 October, and get an extra **4%** in commissions on all of these sales (i.e. if you are on a 10% commission, you'll be paid 14%)
- Show $3000 or more in sales - get an additional **3%**
- Break the $2000 barrier - get an extra **2%**
- Generate $1000 or more in gross sales - get a **$20 GBs** bonus on top of your regular commission

Important: None of the above-quoted October bonuses are excluding our regular cash incentives – we call them GBs or "Geno bucks" – which are:

- **$10.00 GBs** bonus on your second sale with FunToCollect
- **$50.00 GBs** bonus once you've reached a total of $1000 in sales

Simply e-mail me once you've qualified for any of the above (be it sales in October, or datafeed import into your site, or anything else), making sure you include your numerical affiliate ID in the text of the message as well as the bonus you're claiming, and I will credit your account the promised commission increase or GBs bonus(es).

We look forward to your sales and e-mails. Please remember that we are always here to help you perform better with the FunToCollect.com's program.

For your convenience, I am hereby including several links and banners with the tracking codes under each one of them. These codes already have your affiliate ID in them, so all you need to do is cut-n-paste them into the respective space at your website.

Links Embedded With Your Affiliate ID:

Text Link #1
<a href=CODE HERE</a>

Text Link #1
<a href=CODE HERE</a>

Picture of 88x31 static button
<a href=CODE HERE</a>

Picture of 88x31 animated button
<a href=CODE HERE</a>

Picture of 468x60 static banner
<a href=CODE HERE</a>

Picture of 468x60 animated banner
<a href=CODE HERE</a>

Picture of 120x600 static banner
<a href=CODE HERE</a>

Picture of 120x600 animated banner
<a href=CODE HERE</a>

Many more links may be found by logging into your affiliate account at ShareASale here: http://www.shareasale.com/a-login.cfm. Once you've logged in, click on the "Get Links/ Banners / Referral URLs" hyperlink under the "GET LINKS" menu and you'll find FunToCollect's text links and banners there. Please remember that we are also paying $10.00 GBs for loading our datafeed! Our datafeed may also be found under the "GET LINKS" menu quoted above.

Tool of the Month:

Remember that you do not have to possess any programming skills to get our datafeed imported into your website. We offer you a convenient tool that will help you with this, and it is offered absolutely *free of charge*. This tool is our Dynamic Datafeed Template. It can help you put together a website with all the FTC collectibles on it virtually within minutes. The Template is extremely user-friendly and easily customizable to fit your website's current look and style. You may

study the full details of how to use this affiliate tool at
www.funtocollect.net/dynamic-template.php

Should you have any questions regarding the FunToCollect.com's
Affiliate Program, do not hesitate to contact me at
funtocollect@amnavigator.com. I am here to help you and will be
delighted to assist you with anything I can to get you on your way to
success with FunToCollect.

Sincerely yours,

Geno Prussakov
FunToCollect.com Affiliate Manager
dedicated program management by AM Navigator

I am at your service via all IM-chats:
AIM: eprussakov77
ICQ: 207974431
YIM: eprussakov
Skype: eprussakov1

Feel free to modify the above two newsletters to suit your
own affiliate program.

Q.: What do I do if an affiliate does not reply?

A.: An affiliate may not reply for any number of reasons.
According to the information I have gathered, less than half of
the instances for non-reply mean lack of interest! It could be
that your e-mail got caught by spam filters, or because it just
bounced (in either scenario it never got to the intended
recipient). It could also be that the recipient simply forgot
about it. Results of an affiliate poll I conducted in mid-2006
displayed the following:

Not interested	45.45%
Forgotten about it (remind in 3-5 days)	13.64%
Forgotten about it (remind in 7-10 days)	6.82%

Forgotten about it (do not remind)	0.00%
Thinking I'll get to it when I get to it	34.09%

The last four are basically your "forgotten about it" options – just worded differently. To reiterate, fewer than half of affiliates do not reply to you because they are not interested in your offer. 54.55% either do not remember what the offer was, or else procrastinate. This is helpful to know! You simply want to remind them in about a week what your offer was, and perhaps also have an additional incentive attached to the reminder to get them going faster. I would not remind more than one time.

Beware: affiliates are generally annoyed when you request an acknowledgement of message receipt or reading. They are just as perturbed with the affiliate managers who use CAPS in the subjects of their e-mails, or mark them as "High Priority".

Q.: Is it helpful to categorize affiliates?

A.: Extremely! Once your program is up and moving, you will see that some affiliates are doing better than others, and you may want to categorize them differently within your affiliate account, so as to be able to approach them with different offers (e.g.: performance-encouraging bonuses for the active ones, and activation incentives for the passive ones). With time you may also single out a group of preferred affiliates – those that are on some kind of special commission deal. You will be able to customize this categorization yourself. But first and foremost, each affiliate manager should understand that affiliates differ from the very outset (even before they join your affiliate program). I break them down into the following 5 groups (arranging them in an alphabetical order):

- *Content affiliates* – affiliates that build content-saturated sites and feature merchants' banners, links and/or products on the side (may use "Support our website" or "Our sponsors" sections for this)
- *Coupon & rebate affiliates* – affiliates that play on human psychology of trying to find something at a discounted price if possible. The coupon type would put together collections of coupons from different merchants, while the rebate type would offer customers cash-backs (naturally, of lower percentage than the commission they are getting from the merchant).
- *Malls* – affiliates that sell products of multiple merchants (often not united by any subject) "under one roof". A sub-group of *price comparison affiliates* should definitely be mentioned here. Adding the convenient tool of cross-merchant price-check to their online malls, they add value to it, simplifying the product search and comparison process for the end user.
- *Niche affiliates* – affiliates that only specialize on a particular niche (or niches), and optimize their website in such a way that it gets most of that targeted traffic. Examples of popular affiliate niches are: apparel, shoes, tobacco & alcohol, sports.
- *Pay-per-click affiliates* – affiliates that bid on merchant-specific keywords and keyphrases at Google, Yahoo!, MSN and other search engines, and either send the PPC traffic directly to the merchant's website or via an in-between page of their own (depending on their own goals and the restrictions imposed by the merchant).

The above list does not include those that I call want-to-be-affiliates (banner farms is the best example). Each of the above groups has its super affiliates, meaning affiliates capable of generating a significant volume of sales for an affiliate program. You need to understand the way each group works, what problems and challenges they encounter, what factors they are considering while looking for an affiliate program to join, and what they want you, as an affiliate manager, to help them with once they are on board with your program. The above-quoted Peter the Great example is the best way to learn these things. Start affiliate accounts with all major networks and take your time to try yourself in the capacity of PPC affiliate, mall affiliate, coupon affiliate, etc. You will gain invaluable experience in the process. Do not quit those accounts. Keep promoting the programs you have chosen to promote, trying various affiliate tools provided by the networks and third parties. The affiliate industry is dynamic, with new developments occurring daily. If you want your program to be "on top", you need to learn what it takes to be best on both sides of the court: the affiliate manager's side and the affiliate's side.

Q.: Could my program be right for only one type of affiliate?

A.: No. Any program may be promoted by coupon affiliates (if you are offering coupons, or at least a free shipping deal for those customers that spend more than a particular amount in your store), mall affiliates, PPC affiliates, and at least one more group – content affiliates.

I have had a merchant question my decision on approving a coupon site to his affiliate program when he did not run any coupons. That is fine. Let the affiliate decide whether they can feature you at their site. Maybe it is your prices that attracted their attention, or your free shipping, or the number of products on sale. Let the affiliate decide, but if you suspect an affiliate may not be a good match, ask them how they are planning on promoting you. Ask before you say "Your application has been declined".

Q.: What do I do with stagnant affiliates?

A.: Sooner or later every affiliate manager has to face it - most affiliates on board the affiliate program are inactive. Some have christened it a 5-80 Rule: 5% of your affiliates do 80% of the work. My own observations support this theorem. As already mentioned above, the number of active affiliates on board the affiliate programs I manage fluctuates from 3.5% to 14%. Why are the rest of them stagnant? Haven't they initially signed up for a reason? Yes, they have, and this is a great point from which to start. Approach them! For starters, offer them activation bonuses. Have a qualifying deadline for the activation bonuses. Without time-sensitiveness, promotions do not work as well. Activation promos based on bonuses normally work well for the idle affiliates, as they then know that they are paid for putting up those links. After receiving all of the feedback from those that become active, and rewarding with bonuses, announce how many affiliates got the bonuses and start a new motivational promotion. It can either be based on an extension of the deadline for those that have not yet gotten active, or it can be an entirely new campaign. For instance, you may run a promo where the first sale that occurs by a particular date (say, within the 30 days of the announcement) qualifies the formerly stagnant affiliate for any of the following:

- Double commission for the 30 or so days following the first sale

- Cash prize on top of the affiliate's regular commission
- Lifetime commission increase
- Combination of a commission increase and a cash prize
- Some tangible prize (it can be one of the products you are selling)
- Lifetime increase of the cookie life
- Combination of cookie life and commission increase, or any combination of the above

Once the campaign is finished, you may run something else, or perhaps offer those that have remained passive a commission increase just for putting up their links. They may show idle or stagnant on your affiliate list for two reasons: (i) they have not yet put your banners/links up, or (ii) the links are up, but that webpage gets such little traffic that those links are simply never clicked. The latter is the reason why I would not recommend offering too much cash or considerable commission increases to all passive affiliates. It is okay to offer cash or commission and cookies increase on second sales for all affiliates. The first sale may be driven by the affiliate himself/herself. I have seen this happen when affiliates would buy a $4.95 item with free shipping to get a $50 first sale bonus. When they do this to the merchant, they might as well say, "What a foolish merchant you are; I will use this to get your product at your expense, and will also have a little extra cash on top of it!" Needless to say, this does not cultivate sound business relationships. This is the reason why many merchants do not offer first sale bonuses, or do not make them as large as their second sale bonuses.

Work with those stagnant affiliates at least once a month. Besides running the above-quoted campaigns, take your time to look through their websites and give them practical advice on where you believe your product(s) will fit in with them. They simply may not know the scope of your inventory and may believe that you do not really fit into their business model, website, or their priorities. Offer them not only practical placement advice, but also custom creatives to match their website(s). Be flexible, motivating and reachable.

Q.: How do I motivate my affiliates?

A.: The last section of this book will help you with practical ideas. Besides those, I would encourage you to open affiliate accounts on all major affiliate networks and then join your competitor's affiliate programs, signing up for their newsletters. Also join the in-house affiliate programs your competitors run, requesting to be notified of any and all promotions. As in any kind of marketing, competition analysis and monitoring is an essential part of good affiliate marketing. Monitor what your competitors do, and ensure that your program offers at least equally attractive (or preferably, *much more* attractive!) affiliate conditions, promotions, bonuses, prizes, commission increases, etc, etc.

Q.: How do I create datafeeds?

A.: If your own webmaster is of no assistance, hire a PHP programmer to help you with this. The task itself is not at all complicated, and the whole project will cost you anywhere from $20 to $100. The programmer would have to write a script that pulls all of the necessary data from your site's database. A datafeed file is then created in the requested format that you could then pick from your server (if the feed-generating script resides on your server) and upload it to the affiliate network, or else offer it to your affiliates directly.

Q.: What are parasites & Parasiteware™?

A.: The affiliate marketing term "parasite" and the related "Parasiteware™" – coined by Haiko de Poel, Jr. of ABestWeb.com – certainly stems from the respective biological term designating an organism that lives in or on another living organism, existing at the expense of the latter. Parasiteware™ is a term that includes so-called browser helpers, plug-ins, toolbars, pop-ups, pop-unders, and other BHOs (browser helping objects). These cause affiliate cookies to be overwritten and/or affiliate links to be intercepted or redirected, thereby removing the possibility of proper credit being given to an affiliate in the instance of a sale.

Parasitic applications are essentially a type of adware or software, integrated into or packaged with a program. Initially, programmers used them to bundle adware into their application to help cut the costs of their software development and publishing. With time, the idea started being used by the applications in question. Besides being called Parasiteware™, these software applications are also referred to as Spyware, Theftware, Scumware, and other similar names. Certain merchants are known for their "collaboration" with the operators of such applications in an effort to "cut the investments" into their affiliate marketing endeavors.

Q.: What BHOs should I be aware of?

A.: The following is not a complete list (as new "developments" spring up almost daily), but it is a good place to start: 7FaSSt, AccessPlugin, ActualNames, ACXInstall, AdBreak, AdultLinks, AproposMedia, Aornum, ASpam, AutoSearch, BargainBuddy, BDE, BookedSpace, BrowserAid, BrowserToolbar, Bulla, ClickTheButton, ClientMan, CnsMin, CometCursor, Comload, CommonName, CoolWebSearch, CrackedEarth, CustomToolbar, Cytron, DailyWinner,

DialerOffline, DialerActiveX, DialXS, DownloadPlus, DownloadReceiver, DownloadWare, E2Give, eStart, eXactSearch, ezCyberSearch, ezSearching, FavoriteMan, FlashTrack, FreeScratchAndWin, Gratisware, GlobalNetcom, HotBar, Httper, HuntBar, IEAccess, IEMonit, IEPlugin, IETray, IGetNet, ILookup, InetSpeak, InternetOptimizer, InternetWasher, IPInsight, ISTbar, KeenValue, LinkReplacer, lop, MagicControl, MarketScore, MasterDialer, MatrixDialer, MediaUpdate, Meridian, MoneyTree, MyPageFinder, MySearch, NavExcel, nCase, NetPal, Network Essentials, NewDotNet, NewtonKnows, NowBox, Onflow, OnlineDialer, PerMedia, PowerStrip, Pugi, RapidBlaster, SaveNow, SCBar, SearchAndBrowse, Searchex, SearchSquire, SearchWWW, ShopNav, SmartBrowser, SpyBlast, StarDialer, StripPlayer, SubSearch, Surfairy, SuperBar, SVAPlayer, TinyBar, ToolbarCC, TopText, TOPicks, Transponder, Wazam, webHancer, Whazit, Winshow, Winupie, Wonderland, XDialer, XDiver, XLoader, Xupiter, ZeroPopUp, Zipclix, Zyncos.

Q.: What spyware operators should I be aware of?

A.: Again, we are not claiming to have a complete listing, as the Internet is so dynamic that such a claim is virtually impossible. The following is a good list of names you need to be aware of: 180solutions (MetricsDirect), Aluria Software, Box Tops 4 Education, Claria (Gator), CommissionMaker, e2Give, eBates, Ezula, HuntBar, iGive, Kaaza, Keyword Media, MyPoints , PointsPassport, PurityScan, SchoolCash, SchoolPop, Search Engine Stuff, ShopatHomeSelect, Upromise, WhenU, WurldMedia.

Wikipedia's summary on the subject is eloquent and clear:

> Spyware which attacks affiliate networks does so by placing the spyware operator's affiliate tag on the user's activity—replacing

any other tag, if there is one. This harms just about everyone involved in the transaction other than the spyware operator. The user is harmed by having their choices thwarted. A legitimate affiliate is harmed by having their earned income redirected to the spyware operator. Affiliate marketing networks are harmed by the degradation of their reputation. Vendors are harmed by having to pay out affiliate revenues to an "affiliate" who did not earn them through a contractual agreement.

Q.: What are good resources for self-education on spyware issues?

A.: Ben Edelman's (www.benedelman.org) and Kellie Stevens' (www.affiliatefairplay.com) publications are of value. Also, their seminars and websites would be the other resources I would highly recommend for every affiliate manager's continuing education on the subject.

Q.: Isn't affiliate marketing dead/dying?

A.: Every once in a while you will see a forum post, a broadcast, or an article where a claim is made that affiliate marketing is dead or dying. It isn't true. Yes, things have gotten more complex with time. The competition between affiliates has become stiffer, as the number of affiliates has increased with affiliate marketing spreading around the globe. However, this very affiliate competition is refining affiliates, themselves. They admit the need for continuous education and for keeping up to date in the ever-so-changing world of Internet technologies. Those who are not afraid of investing and working hard day by day are still making good money. I mean really good money; some of them - hundreds of thousands of dollars a month. The same is true for merchants. As long as they keep investing wisely and learning continuously, they succeed. Leave the philosophy of this question to theoreticians, and start practicing. You will soon see for yourself that affiliate marketing is alive and well.

Q.: What do I do if my affiliates put their personal orders through their accounts?

A.: I am often asked this question by my clients and my reply always goes like this: I always recommend allowing this, as this only increases their interest as well as your own business. However, if you are giving away first sale bonuses (with some of my clients they run as large as $50!), I would suggest entering them into the program's TOS (or the program's conditions for the first sale bonus awarding), that *only* first sales from customers qualify.

Q.: How can a SWOT analysis help?

A.: Having used the SWOT analysis in my own work, I believe it to be extremely handy while planning any affiliate program's future. SWOT is a strategic planning model that helps the researcher analyze where the object of his/her study is currently, where it is desired to be, and the best way of getting there. For this purpose, the Strengths, Weaknesses, Opportunities and Threats are laid out in four quadrants, forming the following SWOT matrix:

Strengths *Good Present* Maintain, build, leverage	Weaknesses *Bad Present* Remedy, stop
Opportunities *Good Future* Prioritize, optimize	Threats *Bad Future* Minimize

There are three steps that you need to take in the strategic planning of your affiliate program:

1 – Determine where you are now. Start this by listing all of the strengths of your affiliate program, then turning to the weaknesses, listing them in the respective section of your matrix.

2 – Foresee where you might be in the future. Again, start from the good, listing all of the opportunities that may exist in the future. Next, turn to the threats, and list your potential future weaknesses.

3 – Prepare a plan of action. Based on your own SWOT matrix, put together an action plan that addresses each of the four areas reflected in the matrix. In your action plan, aim at maintaining the *strengths* (building upon them and leveraging them), remedying the *weaknesses*, prioritizing and optimizing the *opportunities*, and minimizing the *threats*

Part 2
Affiliate Manager
& Merchant Mistakes

You must learn from the mistakes of others. You can't possibly live long enough to make them all yourself.

Sam Levenson

When the thought of writing this book first crossed my mind, I started thinking about its format and decided to make it follow the pattern of questions and answers. As I worked my way through the most frequently asked merchant and affiliate managers' questions, I bumped into a group of queries that were searching for an all-encompassing answer to the same issue: how to build a bullet-proof, 100% affiliate-satisfying, successful affiliate program. To stress the positive, I started digging into the negative. What do affiliates dislike? What practices should affiliate managers and merchants avoid at all costs? I even attempted to spell out the all-encompassing answer to the question that so many affiliate managers and merchants want to know. However, the more I wrote, the larger the answer became. With progress, the question-and-answer format became inappropriate, and my long answer to one question grew into a book section of its own. I entitled it: "Affiliate Manager & Merchant Mistakes".

I see mistakes committed on three fronts. All of these fronts are to be closely monitored and kept flawless for a merchant who wants to run a successful affiliate marketing campaign. These three fronts are (i) the affiliate program itself, (ii) the merchant's website, and (iii) the daily affiliate management. As time passes and your experience grows, your list of affiliate-unfriendly practices will also expand. Write them down and review them regularly, so as to avoid the path that leads to destruction of an affiliate program. You will find out that much of your time will be spent on affiliate recruitment. But this is only the beginning. You'll want to know the problems that you may run into, and how to avoid inadvertently creating obstacles for your affiliates. In short, you ultimately want your affiliates to keep sending you those sales so you can make some money along the way.

Refine your affiliate management skills daily. Study diligently, and you will inevitably succeed! The famous

English author and critic of the 18th century Samuel Johnson wrote: "Few things are impossible to diligence and skill. Great works are performed not by strength, but perseverance." Persevere in perfecting your affiliate management practices. Use the section below to help you with your endeavors.

In what follows you will find one hundred actual mistakes committed by merchants and affiliate managers – including some made by the author of this book. And this is okay. It is how we learn. Hugh Lawson White, a US politician and president pro tempore of Senate 1832, wrote: "When you make a mistake, don't look back at it long. Take the reason of the thing into your mind and then look forward. Mistakes are lessons of wisdom. The past cannot be changed. The future is yet in your power." It is to the brighter future of the affiliate marketing world that I devote this chapter.

1
Mistakes Made
Within the Affiliate Program

AM's That Do Not Know Their Business. Many affiliates are highly professional in what they do and know their industry very well. Some of them even get offers to manage merchant's affiliate programs. As in any industry, amateur workers pretending to be professionals are generally not welcomed and may be treated with disregard. Do not give them reason to do this to you. Educate yourself daily, ask questions, read, and attend relevant conferences and seminars. Practice everything you learn. There will be a direct correlation between your own professional growth and the growing respect your affiliates will have for you.

Embarrassing Commission Rates (1-2%). Once you have started your program and are ready to have affiliates join and promote you, do not insult them with embarrassingly low commission rates. Your goal is to attract serious affiliates. Though you may be selling expensive merchandise, keep in mind that even diamond and gold-selling stores set their affiliate programs' commissions at 5% to 10%. Do not scare away a good affiliate base by offering embarrassing commission rates.

Commission Drops. Let us say, for example, your original commission was set at 15%. With time you realize that this is more than you can afford to pay, and you make the decision to lower that commission rate to 10%. It is no exaggeration when I tell you that this move could very well bury your affiliate program! Think of it this way: you just cut your affiliates' pay by one third. Regardless of the fact that your affiliates are not your employees, imagine for a moment that a similar situation happened to you at work, where you were hired to work for $90,000 a year, but failed to notice the fine print in your contract that stated the employer could alter the terms of the agreement as seen fit. At the end of the first few months, everything looked fine, and you were paid your $7,500 each month. At the end of the fourth month however, you realized that both for the third and the fourth month, you were paid only $5,000 for each of these months. Would a paycheck cut of one-third make you a happy camper? More than likely you would break that contract and be on your way to find employment elsewhere. With affiliates, the outcome of "finding employment elsewhere" is more sobering to the merchant than in the above-quoted employee-employer example. Affiliates have the traffic important to the merchants, and when insulted by any of the means spoken of in this section, will more than likely replace *your* links and products on their website with *your competitor*'s links and products. Please keep this in mind as you read through the rest of this section.

Insignificant Return Days. I know of a merchant that sells several *wonderful* lines of products, has a great website, and pays a generous commission. However, in the place where other merchants typically have a "return days" question and answer in their Affiliate FAQs, this merchant has the following question and answer:

> **How does XYZ.com track users that come from my web site?**
> When a customer clicks to XYZ.com via a link that you have created ..., XYZ.com will track any merchandise purchases that a customer makes so that we can credit your account appropriately. This tracking activity persists until the customer closes his or her browser. Tracking will also cease if the customer does not click on a link at XYZ.com for 45 minutes or more. [*text taken from the merchant's website, replacing the merchant's name by XYZ.com*]

How many return days? Not even a day! Once that browser window is closed or the end user spends "45 minutes or more" on the merchant's website, the affiliate gets nothing. This is not a good practice if your intent is to honor your affiliate. The merchant in this case clearly does not understand how much work often has to be done just to send one prospective customer to their website. This particular policy shows that, regardless of the words on crediting the affiliate account "appropriately", they are adding two additional conditions which make the *appropriate* crediting – as understood by a predominant number of affiliates and affiliate managers – entirely impossible. Learn from the mistakes of others, and do not repeat them in your own affiliate program.

Unclear Commission Structure. If the commission paid to affiliates is tied to the monetary volume of sales, clarify this in the program's description, spelling it out in a straightforward table of *sales volume – commission* correlations. Do not simply say: "We pay up to 25% commissions". Tell them what they have to do to get the 25%. As one affiliate has puts it: "Don't tell me it's up to the magical affiliate fairy to decide whether I get 5% or 25%". Be transparent and clear from the start. Here is an example of how performance-based commission increases are spelled out by a jewelry merchant:

MONTHLY SALES	COMMISSION
$0 - $5,000	8%
$5,001 - $10,000	10%
$10,001 and up	12%

Important: If the commission quoted in the second column is paid to affiliates on a graduated tier structure, do specify this so as to avoid misunderstanding. If we use the above example, the graduated tier structure would presuppose an 8% commission on the first monthly batch of $5,000, then 10% on the second batch of $5000, and 12% on all sales above $10,000.

I do understand that the above pattern of spelling the rules out may not work for every affiliate program. Some merchants offer smaller commissions on one type of product and a much larger one on another. If your affiliate program does that, be as concrete as possible on how this works. Here is an example of how an ink affiliate program that pays "up to 25%" in commissions explains such a pattern:

Monthly Revenue	Cmptbl	Reman Ink	Reman Combo	Reman Toner	Refill Kits	OEM	Other
$0 - $2,499	21%	7%	3%	5%	22%	0.5%	5%
$2,500 - $4,999	22%	8%	4%	6%	23%	1%	6%
$5,000 - $7,999	23%	9%	5%	7%	24%	1.75%	7.5%
$8,000 - $9,999	24%	10.25%	5.75%	8%	24.5%	2.5%	9%
$10,000+	25%	12%	6.75%	10%	25%	3%	10%

The motto, as always, is: "be transparent and clear". If you are not, it may be assumed you are not trustworthy – an assumption you definitely want to avoid.

Unrealistic Goals for Commission Increases. If you want to offer a performance-based commission increase, it is best to set realistic goals for your affiliates. Do not promise them a 1% commission increase if they reach $10,000 in sales within the next 30 days, or within any given month. Make it enchanting and encouraging; not insulting and depressive.

Vague and/or Missing Conditions. Whatever you do, state your conditions fully and clearly at the very outset. Do not send out private commission offers, then announce these offers are conditional only once the new affiliates have signed up. Do not start promotions, contests, or any other campaigns until you have refined and thoroughly thought through the conditions that need to be satisfied by affiliates for the campaign to work for you

Commission Increases at the Expense of Cookie Duration & Visa Versa. Do not tie the increase of any of these variables to the decrease of the other. When you increase the commission level two-fold, while shortening the cookie duration by half, it does not look like you are playing the game honestly. When you decide to increase that commission level, increase it, but leave the cookies alone. Lowering the commission level with the increase of the cookies looks even worse.

Unreliable Reporting. Reporting is an extremely important component of your affiliate program. If you are on an affiliate network, make sure they are known for their dependable reporting. If you have chosen to run an "indie", remember that affiliates want to see detailed and unswerving hits and sales reports in it, too. Remember also that affiliates will perform test purchases themselves, and heaven forbid one of them doesn't track! If this happens, they will spread the word around faster than you can blink, and your affiliate program will be at risk, not to mention your reputation in the business.

Payment Processing Fees. If you choose to run your affiliate program on an affiliate network, ensure they have direct deposit and check-in-the-mail available as payment methods (both without any additional charges to the affiliate). The same applies to running an in-house affiliate program. You may charge for international payouts, and overseas affiliates would generally not mind it at all. However, for within-the-country payments, I advise you to flee from those payment processing fees as much as from the program sign-up fees.

Automatic Rejections of Non-US-Based Affiliates. This can be a tremendous mistake, and unfortunately, this still happens with some affiliate programs that are being run. Never assume that because an affiliate is based outside of the United States, that this automatically means s/he can be of no use to you. According to the statistics published at the InternetWorldStats.com for the year 2006, North America's share in the world's Internet traffic only amounts to 21.09%. Many of you may already have one foot out the door to pull up the latest data on USA online trade. There's no need – I'll help you out. The United States accounts for close to 50% of the world's money spent online. However, affiliates outside of the U.S. can be a great asset to your program. Many of them have excellent organic traffic – often highly targeted and interesting to you as a merchant. As an example, I want to turn to the facts about some of the US programs I manage. One of my best collectibles-selling affiliates is in UK, while the other one is in Switzerland; a Dutch and a Canadian are in the top 10 of my ink affiliates; an Indian and one from China are in the top 20 of a magazine merchant. The list of the top 50 affiliates of another collectibles merchant of mine contains affiliates from Singapore, Serbia and Montenegro, Malaysia, South Africa and again Canada, United Kingdom, India, and the Netherlands. I believe this illustrates my point well.

Parasites. See the respective question and answer above. Fight parasites. Constantly educate yourself and your merchant/client about them, and follow the latest tendencies in this sector of the industry. Become known as a parasite-fighter, and serious affiliates will appreciate your stand.

Expired Coupons. Each coupon should have an expiration date. Affiliates do not like open-dated coupons. However, when you set the coupon expiry date, please remember to remove that coupon from the list of those still available (if your affiliate software or affiliate network does not do this by itself). It does not show good affiliate program management when a program shows outdated coupons as still available.

Difficult Coupon Codes. Do not make coupon codes overly complex. Remember that a coupon code should fit and be readable on a coupon banner. For example, do not make yours look like this: wwwxyziiivyeir75ee, or anything of the kind. Let them make sense (e.g.: if you are offering 15 off on all scooters in the shop, make the coupon you are going to offer through affiliates look something like this: SCT15OFF). Also try not to use 0 (zero) next to O (capital letter "o"), and l (small letter "L" next to 1 (one); better yet, exclude them from coupon codes altogether to avoid any confusion. In addition, avoid spelling your coupon codes in lower case letters (e.g.: sct15off, Sct15Off). There should also be no special characters ($, %, _, #, &, etc.) in them. Stick with numbers and upper case letters. If your shopping cart allows it, make your coupon codes recognizable by it regardless of how they were entered: in lower or upper case.

Confusing Coupons. When you publish a coupon, ensure there is nothing confusing about it. Each coupon should have a clear expiration date. Refrain from using "no expiration

115

date" coupons unless the deal you are offering really is ongoing and you can support it "for life". It should also have a correct affiliate link, full and straightforward details, and a simple, non-confusing coupon code. If any of these lack from the coupon published, affiliates may not even look at it. Besides the above-quoted points, you want to make sure there are no rigid restrictions tied to how and whom may use the coupon, and, by all means, test the coupon before you start offering it to your affiliates (it has to work!).

Belated Coupon Announcements. This applies to any and all promotions run by your affiliate program. Always notify your affiliates of seasonal or other promotions well in advance so they can upload the new links. Remember that you are not the only merchant they are promoting, and the longer you procrastinate with the promo notification, the less chance you have of being promoted properly. History has also seen merchants notifying affiliates of seasonal promotions after the event/holiday has already taken place. Need I say more?

Promo Extensions without Prior Notice. Extending a good promo may work fine, as long as you notify your affiliates of the extension in advance – before they pull down those links. Just as always, think of it as if you were in the affiliate's shoes. Notify them at least a couple of days before the initial expiration date approaches.

Frequently Repeated Coupons. Even if you are offering an extremely great bargain during one month, do not offer it repeatedly over a long period of time. This builds expectation on the part of the customer/consumer, and the promo loses its effectiveness.

116

Furnishing Affiliates With "Less-Than" Coupons. When you put together affiliate coupons, ensure you are not already offering better deals at your own website directly to your visitors. Coupons provided for affiliates to use should be at least as attractive (and preferably, even more motivating!) as the coupons you offer to customers directly.

If you cannot come up with coupons that are better than what you already offer, then at least do not restrict the affiliates' use of coupons only to those that are provided to them directly.

Inaccessible Creatives. If you run a promotion campaign and have creatives to go with the promo, remember to include these creatives in your promotional e-mail, and to also make them accessible to your affiliates via your general inventory of creatives. If you do not do this, each affiliate's participation in the promo will be at the mercy of that "Delete" button (once the e-mail with your promotional creatives is gone from their sight, your program is out of their mind).

Insufficient Creative Support. Be it a coupon you are publishing or a new line of products, you want your affiliates to start promoting. Put together a nice selection of different sized banners and buttons to help make this happen. *Also* make yourself available to accommodate any custom banner requests. Remember Napoleon Hill's words: "You can start right where you stand and apply the habit of going the extra mile by rendering more service and better service than you are now being paid for."

Creatives Abnormalities. Here I would like to mention creatives of unbearably large file sizes, creatives with no width, height, or alt tags, and creatives not meeting the affiliate banners' guidelines mentioned in the Launch section above.

Absence of Holiday-Related Creatives. Any affiliate program can and should have these. Even if you are in a translation and interpreting business, you can make Thanksgiving and Christmas-related coupon banners (your actual gift is then the discount the end user gets) for your affiliates to offer at their websites. Holidays are great reasons to market your product/service. Use them as opportunities for promotion. When you make your holiday creatives, ensure you have them for *all* major holidays of the targeted country.

Strange Characters in Your Datafeed. Keep these away from your datafeed. Characters like &, ", >, %, !, #, @, ~, &nsbp; and those that are not your regular text should be kept out of datafeeds.

Datafeeds With No Categories. It is okay to have one or even no categories if all you are selling is, let's say, eight camera bags. But if your datafeed contains hundreds or even dozens of products from different categories, and you have put that datafeed together for affiliates to use it, have those categories in place. Most affiliates will not even work with a no-category datafeed.

Datafeed Product Images of One Size. Some merchants would pre-suppose that affiliates should have a way of converting the large files they supply in their datafeed to thumbnails. Trust me, affiliates do not appreciate this. Neither do they appreciate having *only* thumbnails in their datafeed. Do not presume. Just give them large images for the close-ups, and small images for thumbnails.

Identical Product Descriptions. There are some merchants who have identical product description (at least in the first 250 characters) for each product in their datafeed. This is sometimes conditioned by the fact that this data is pulled from the merchant's database, which really has each product description start in the same way, then lists the differences later on in the text. Keep in mind that affiliates may not have more than 200-250 character spaces for each product description! List such important parameters as dimensions, color, material that the product is made of, and other product-specific characteristics in the very beginning of the description you are providing to your affiliates.

Frequent Datafeed Changes. If you are going to make any major change in your datafeed, talk to your affiliates before you start. Ask them for feedback. Find out what other things they would want to see changed and/or added to it. Next, implicate the changes, alert them that you are about to upload the new feed, upload it, and notify them that the new feed is available. Do not apply any major changes to your datafeed too frequently. Adding new products, deleting the ones that went out of stock, refining product descriptions, and adding product-specific keywords into a custom field are all fine. What I mean by major changes are mainly changes in category and subcategory names and groupings.

Datafeeds with Out-of-stock Items that are Not Expected to Return. If a product is sold-out and is not expected to come back, delete if from the datafeed. Make sure you keep the thumbnail image of the product or have it replaced with a "sold out" image of the thumbnail size, but do not keep the product information in the datafeed if there is no hope for it to come back. Otherwise, you will end up with a lot of sold-out products in your datafeed, affiliates will keep featuring them on their websites, and the end result will be disappointed prospective customers.

Datafeeds with Outdated Prices. Some merchants choose not to have the prices in their datafeeds, others are required to have them there by their affiliate network. If you do have prices mentioned in your datafeed, make sure you update them in that feed as frequently as you update them on the website; and notify your affiliates of the new prices datafeed availability in a timely manner. If this is not done, sooner or later you will run into problems with customers that will tell you of your product being featured on the Internet at much lower prices, and asking you to honor those prices. Merchants with datafeeds should also remember to recommend to their datafeed affiliates that they either (i) automatically update their datafeeds/websites, or (ii) do not display prices.

Datafeeds with Useless Data. Ensure that yours does not contain any information that is not directly related to the way your affiliate is going to use a product. You do not have to include all possible information in it - just what will be useful for your affiliates and required by the datafeed specifications.

Micro-Categorized Datafeeds. In trying to do their best with the categorization of products, select merchants may micro-categorize them to such an extent that some of the categories end up having only one or two products in them, with no way to unite them into larger, more embracing categories. It may be of help to your affiliates if you only create categories and subcategories, limiting the number of larger categories to such a quantity that gives affiliates a chance to choose for themselves. They may then choose to go with a larger category that has an assortment of products from narrower subcategories, or else use your finer categorization.

Product ID's or SKU's Missing from Datafeeds. Many affiliates do need these to separate between the products of different merchants within one website. It isn't that hard to include them in your datafeed. Do not presume they are unnecessary pieces of information.

Changing Product ID's or SKU's. This point is mainly directed specifically at affiliate networks, but you as a merchant should also remember to keep the same product ID or SKU for each product from datafeed to datafeed, regardless of the time of the year.

Uploading Old Datafeeds. Do not play with the idea of uploading your same old datafeed to the network just to get that "last updated" date refreshed and replaced by a newer one. Affiliates that have their notifications or software fetches set up at catching all datafeed updates will be extremely disappointed by finding out nothing changed, and that they just spent their time on what they already had uploaded.

Lack of Deep Links. Having all links leading to the homepage of the merchant's website is a big mistake - it shows a lack of understanding on how many affiliates work. The best affiliates are those sales people of yours that not only post your link at their website, but post it in such a way that it adds value both to their website and to yours. If you sell hundreds or even thousands of products from different categories, spend your time creating good deep-linked affiliate creatives and text links. If the software (or the affiliate network) you are using allows your affiliates to generate deep links themselves, this will certainly ease your job. However, you would still want to have a few good links as examples.

Lack of Individual Product or Category Links. If you are selling multiple products, try your best to make a datafeed available to your affiliates. If, however, for some reason you cannot make one available to them, either provide them with a way to create product links, or make yourself available to create these for them. The same applies to category links. Some affiliates may only be interested in either linking to specific products or specific product categories. Do not assume that linking to your homepage will suffice. Not giving them a chance to get the links they need will eventually deprive you of the traffic and sales they may send you.

Broken Links. Keep an eye on the links you offer to your affiliates, and if any of them become invalid, not working, or broken, either try to fix them, or at least notify your affiliates of the problem before their website visitors start complaining.

Other Landing Page Problems. Besides 404 File Not Found errors, these also include product links leading to entirely different products when the link is actually clicked. Test how your datafeed works before you offer it to affiliates.

Code Altering Restrictions. I would not recommend demanding that your affiliates   stick with the HTML-code that you provide them. After all, what matters for *you* is that a sale is sent, and to *them*, that it gets tracked. Do explain why you do not want them to play with that code unless they really know what they are doing, but do not restrict the altering of the code. There may be circumstances when they would want to change it to fit into their context better. Give them the freedom to do this if they so choose.

122

Rigid PPC Restrictions. I have seen some merchants limiting affiliates in their PPC Bidding Rules to such an extent that all of the best-converting top product keywords and key-phrases were kept to the merchant, and bids were allowed only on those that were very generic, or else on those that were poorly-converting. Do not expect to attract any serious PPC affiliate to promote your program if, besides your trademark(s), you have also secured hundreds of other keywords for your own use only.

Brand Image Obsession. If you are promoting the affiliate program of a merchant concerned about the brand image of their company, make the pre-screening of your affiliate applications and websites the first and the most important step in the approval process. However, make sure you are not brand image obsessed in your approach. You should be brand image *focused*, but by no means *obsessed*. By being focused on the brand image, I mean to say that you should view each affiliate website as a potential brick in the building of the brand; however, you should not be too restrictive in your selection process. Do not assume that an affiliate shopping mall or a coupon site will not contribute to the brand-building. Approve these sites into your affiliate program and provide them with top-notch graphics to use, making your brand stand-out amongst other featured brands!

Major Changes in September-December. When that fourth quarter hits, please refrain from any major changes to your affiliate program. It is by far the most important time of the year for most affiliates. Be it changes to the platform your affiliate program is run on, the tracking links, the thumbnail images of the products, or anything else that implies work to be done on the affiliate site – please either make sure these are

123

done either before September starts or after the winter holiday shopping season ends.

Late Notifications of Seasonal Promotions. When you are planning on running a seasonal promotion that is tied to a particular holiday or a series of holidays, remember to notify your affiliates of it well in advance. Some affiliates appreciate being notified as early as possible, preferably a month or two beforehand.

Changes Without Notice. If you have to make a change within your affiliate program – be it a banner, a datafeed, a link change, or anything else – remember to duly notify your affiliates. If possible, explain the reasons behind the change. Be honest yet optimistic in notifications like this. Even if it is not a change but a temporary inactivity of your dynamic template that you have to announce, do it with a smile and an optimistic spirit. There are two ways to notify mall shoppers that the escalator is not working: (i) put a sign on it saying "Temporarily Out of Service", or (ii) put up a sign that says: "This Escalator Temporarily Works as a Stair-Case". The advantages of the second way are obvious. Use this idea in your affiliate notifications.

Program's TOS Copied from the Network's TOS. Previously I mentioned direct one-line references to the affiliate network's TOS as being the only text of merchants' affiliate program agreements. Sometimes even worse cases are registered. Merchants may simply copy the whole network's TOS and paste it into the space provided for the program's own agreement with affiliates. This results in two negative consequences: (i) most of the clauses in the agreement make no sense in the context of that particular merchant (as they were written for the overall network), and

124

as a result (ii) affiliates do not treat that merchant as a serious business partner.

Exclusivity Clause. Some merchants demand exclusivity from their affiliates, not allowing them to promote any competitor of theirs on the same website or webpage. They may even demand "No competitor. Period." One merchant worded it in their affiliate program agreement the following way: "I agree that ... once I use a link that connects to a specific XYZ.com product, I will not sell or advertise that product in any other way, shape or form unless agreed upon by XYZ.com" [prospective affiliate has to tick the "I Agree" box before proceeding with the application; I have replaced the name of the merchant by XYZ.com]. I have never been a supporter of the exclusivity clause in the program's TOS. I would not recommend having it there if you want to attract a wide range of affiliates. If you do decide to have a clause like this, then limiting affiliates to showing no competitor's links on the *same webpage* would be the strictest demand I would advise. Keep in mind, however, that some groups of affiliates will then be immediately dropped out of your prospective affiliates list (example: coupon affiliates), while others – due to a widely-spread affiliate "allergy" to exclusivity clauses – may not even touch your affiliate sign-up form.

Improper Reversals. These could very well kill your affiliate program. Affiliates do understand that some merchants sell products that often get returned, but they also understand that, more often than not, a pair of shoes gets returned for an exchange, and not a return as such. If an exchange happens, do not reverse the affiliate transaction. If the reversal has to be made – be it due to fraud, return of unwanted merchandise, duplicate order, items out of stock, or any other valid reason – explain the reason to the affiliate whose balance gets debited. Do not play risky games with your affiliates. If your program becomes known for excessive reversals with no reasons given, you will lose their trust as well as good affiliates in the process.

First Sale Reversals. In my opinion, these are counterproductive. Imagine how hard an affiliate may have tried (for days, weeks, maybe even months!) to make that first sale a reality. Then, finally, they find the sale notification in their inbox. You have made their day! They are happy regardless of how big or small that sale was. They now have motivation to carry on. If a few days later they get a reversal of that sale, and of the consequent commission, their heart will drop. What I am about to say may sound irrational, but you will see there is method to the madness. I have done the following many times myself, and would recommend you to do it as well. If you need to reverse a first affiliate sale, look at the commission that would be debited from the affiliate account. Then, keeping in mind what I have described above, decide whether it is worth doing. If the amount of that commission is under $20, I would advise not reversing it at all. If you do not reverse it, the affiliate will never know and will keep on working, pushing your affiliate program, while flying on the wings of inspiration. If you do decide to reverse it, the price of getting him/her back on their feet may be substantially larger than what you would have saved on the reversal of such a fundamental sale for that affiliate.

Reversals of "Expected" Sales. I have seen this happen with the affiliate programs I manage time and again. An old-time customer somehow finds an affiliate website where his favorite merchant's products are featured, clicks the link there, and then goes on to purchase from his favorite merchant. That customer then logs into his existing customer account with the merchant, adds items to the shopping cart, places the order through, and in the morning, the merchant sees that a commission has been deducted for that sale. Yes, things like this happen monthly, if not weekly. However, there is no fault with the affiliate, as their job was done correctly. If that affiliate happened to have better search engine rankings on the keywords important to you, he/she only deserves praise and payment for this sale. Do not even think of reversing such sales, even if you had just spoken with this particular customer on the phone a day before the "expected" sale occurred. Play fairly. Pay those who have earned the commission by doing their part of the job correctly.

Test Sales That Do Not Track. Be it online or phone sales (if you have a phone tracking system in place), ensure that nothing slips through the cracks of an imperfect tracking system or a partial customer service. Every affiliate sale should track. If one doesn't track, and it just so happens to be a sale that the affiliate was aware of (either an affiliate's own test sale, or a sale placed by his/her friend that clicked the link on his/her website), this affiliate will be tempted to doubt your integrity.

Problems Logging In. If you are running an in-house program, make sure both your host and the hosting plan you use support sufficient numbers of simultaneous logins into your affiliate database. No affiliate should ever get such error messages as "Too many open sessions" or "Too many connections" with an Access Denied notification.

Low Affiliate Program Balance. Ensure that your program never goes "temporarily offline" or displays a low balance alert to your current and/or prospective affiliates. If you are on an affiliate network, sign up for automatic balance replenishment, and announce it to your affiliates. They will appreciate it, as it guarantees them that they will always be paid for the work they do for you.

2
Mistakes Made
Within the Website
that Runs an Affiliate Program

Leaks. In affiliate marketing, leaks are specifically defined as external links within your website that lead to sites which do not credit your affiliates for the work they perform (as defined by sending you the traffic and potential sales). Some of the most common examples are AdSense units, banner ads, links to sister sites, etc. A telephone number published on your website may also be deemed a leak (in the event of your affiliate program not having a phone tracking mechanism set in place). If you do take phone orders, set-up a phone tracking system. Be fair to your affiliates. Do not let every page of your website – or worse yet, every page of the checkout process within the website – contradict your claims of "crediting affiliate accounts for every sale sent". If you prominently display toll free numbers to place orders over the phone, heed my advice and have a phone tracking set up.

At the end of this brief look at leaks, I would like to give my unsolicited praise to a specific affiliate network. I was utterly and pleasantly surprised with their attitude at the very onset of my dealings with them, and that is why I want to give them a proper credit for caring about their affiliates. Buy.at is a British affiliate network that would *not* make a program go live until they had tested and confirmed that the merchant's customer service people were doing everything they should do to take affiliate-generated orders properly (read: crediting respective affiliates). By promoting this type of work ethic, it is my hope that more affiliate networks will follow suit.

Playing With the Cookies. This has happened with others in the past, and I would like to warn you to stay away from this risky game. Some merchants may send out a newsletter to all customers, asking them to clear their cookies "for security reasons"; while others may instruct customers that go through the checkout process to clear those cookies to see the "best price available". More "sophisticated" merchants may invent subtler mechanisms for cookie-erasing. An example would be cookie-eraser codes that activate upon opening of the merchant's emails. Other merchants may partner with websites that would agree to be paid a smaller commission than the merchant's default commission, yet be featured on the merchant's "Thank You" page as the merchant's official source for rebates or other offers. These merchants would deem it a wise business decision. Affiliates, on the other hand, would unanimously label decisions like these *unethical*.

Do not let thoughts similar to the above ones even cross your mind. If you lose the trust of your affiliate once, you may never ever gain it back. Play a fair game.

"Become Our Affiliate" Link. You obviously need to have this link at the website (preferably on every page), but do not make it stick out in bold-font, different colors, or in any other way. Some affiliates may deem it a cookie-stealer, as your end client could theoretically first become your affiliate, and then get the commission of his/her own sale. Because of the "last affiliate link gets the commission" rule, this allows for the cookie overwriting, and the affiliate that originally sent you the customer gets no pay. Other affiliates would not appreciate it for a different reason. They may believe that having that link sticking out too aggressively could lead to the recruitment of their own competition (read: other affiliates). At the dawn of its affiliate program's existence, one of the websites whose program I am managing had an "Affiliate Program" link both on the top and on the bottom of every page. When conducting one of my regular affiliate surveys on how to improve the program, I had received numerous requests to remove the bold-font link on the top of each webpage and keep the one on the bottom. We did it, then announced it to the affiliates, and I am certain it helped us lay

another brick in the building of my affiliate reputation, and of that particular program's success.

Having said all this, let me stress that the "Become Our Affiliate" or "Affiliate Program" link *should* be on the merchant's website. Do not go to the other extreme – removing the link from your website altogether, or burying it so deep into your website that it is difficult to find. Make it easily-locatable by those that, upon visiting your website, may think of promoting you at their affiliate sites, through their newsletters, or in any other affiliate way.

Unclear Linking to the Affiliate Sign-up Page. If your affiliate program is with LinkShare, for example, make sure your program bio page (i.e. the page within your website that describes your affiliate program) has a sign-up link directing to the sign-up page of *your affiliate program* at LinkShare, not to the LinkShare's general affiliate sign-up page. Doing so could annoy those affiliates that are already registered with LinkShare.

Lack of Company Description. Affiliates will need to use a description at their websites to introduce your business to their visitors. Either provide them with one that you want them to use, or make sure you have a description on your own website that they can easily copy-and-paste into theirs ("easily" means plain text, not text typed up in a Flash presentation or any other graphics!)

Poor Navigation. Affiliates will often point this out to you. Neither you as a merchant, nor they as your salespeople, are interested in promoting a website that is poorly navigated. The Three-Click Rule is a good one to follow: this recommends that any page within the website is able to be located within a three-clicks distance from the homepage. The number of clicks does not always have to be exactly three, however, the principle of keeping an "intuitive, logical hierarchical structure" (cf. Jeffrey Zeldman's "Taking Your Talent to the Web" book) is *essential* for a website that wants to be successful in e-commerce.

Bad Product Images. As one affiliate puts it, these refer to "product images that look like they were taken with a Polaroid with low batteries in a red light district penny theater". Affiliates care about quality product photos. You will often find them to be your most constructive critics, and if they intend to promote you seriously, they will also examine your website closely. If the truth be known, this evaluation of "serious promotion" often takes place after they sign-up for the program, not before. If you do not accommodate their requests for bettering your website swiftly and profoundly, they may just walk away. It takes a lot of effort to find good affiliates – do what it takes to keep them.

Unlicensed Product Images. If you offer a datafeed or specific product links, remember that those product images will be displayed on the websites of your affiliates. Heaven forbid you use unlicensed images on your website or in the creatives you are supplying to your affiliates! The consequences could be dreadful.

Slow Load Time. The website load time is important for affiliates. As you may know, it is affected by several factors, including the size of the webpages that the website consists of, the complexity of those webpages, the responsiveness and location of the host's servers, and, finally, the Internet connection speed of the end-user. Tools like WebPageAnalyzer.com can give you any webpage's download time on various connections (from a 14.4k modem

134

connection to a T1 1.44Mbps one). Statistics show that 1/3 of visitors will not wait for more than 8-10 seconds for a webpage to load. Keep this in mind and optimize your webpages accordingly. Some affiliates will not even bother sending the traffic to you if they know that 30+% of the visitors they send to you will not see your website. A rule of thumb is that on a 56k connection every page of your website loads within 12 seconds or less.

Spelling Mistakes. No additional comment required.

Unclear Product Descriptions. This relates to all kinds of products and all kinds of merchants. If you have not had good product descriptions before starting your affiliate program, you will be forced to get them up once you start getting complaints about them from you affiliates. In a way, it is a good reason to finally get these done, but I would certainly recommend you have them ready before starting the affiliate program.

Non-Competitive Prices. Once you have entered the world of affiliate marketing as a merchant, you have exposed your website to thousands of experienced Internet marketers, where it will be seen in bright light. Non-competitive prices will be pointed out to you by affiliates; do not reply to them that the reason they are so high is "so that you are able to pay them their commission". One fairly new affiliate program I manage has some of the best-priced products in their segment, and regardless of the commission level only being set at 10% (while its competitors are offering as much as 15%), it converts *much* better for its affiliates than the competing affiliate programs that have been there for several years. Non-competitive prices are never justified in the long

135

run. High-priced products result in lower affiliate conversions. Remember this.

3
Day-To-Day Affiliate Program
Management Mistakes

Charging to Join Your Program. The predominant number of affiliate programs nowadays do not entail any joining fees. Do not make yours the exception by charging fees to join, or you will instantly kill affiliates' interest in your program. Affiliate marketing, as any marketing, is *your* investment, not theirs; and regardless of the popularity of your brand, I would not recommend charging affiliates to join your program.

Belated Approvals. If membership to your program is available by manual approval only, please remember that you must look through those affiliate websites and either qualify or disqualify them from joining your affiliate program. Do not delay the approval decision of any affiliate application for longer than 5 business days. The best practice, of course, is to review and approve affiliates on a daily basis.

Information Missing from Approval E-mails. We have already discussed the necessity of having the affiliate network information (if the affiliate program is not an in-house one) in the approval e-mail, but I would also like to address this again here. Far too many AM's commit this mistake, sending out approval messages with no mention of the affiliate network details. To start putting up your links, the affiliate would then have to go to your website, find the page describing your affiliate program, and get the information on the network from there. In the course of doing so, they are losing precious time that they could be spending putting up links. Value your affiliates' time and let this be reflected in your approval email.

Untargeted Recruitment E-mails. If you are contacting a particular website with a proposal to join your affiliate program, and your recruitment e-mail is geared towards websites in a specific vertical, filter your list of targets carefully before you e-mail that proposal (read: "Potential Affiliates"). Otherwise, you may end up sending out affiliate recruitment e-mails for a makeup merchant to websites that specialize exclusively in motor oil sales. Needless to say, you may not be treated seriously even if that particular affiliate happens to have a skin care website as well.

Asking for Something you Cannot Return. One of the ideas that may work wonderfully for the development of your affiliate program is asking a non-competing merchant from a related vertical to join your affiliate program and place the link on their "Thank You" page. If you are selling chewing gum, it may be a dental care merchant; if you are selling sports equipment, it may be a sports shoes merchant, and so on. However, prior to asking another merchant for something like this, put yourself into their shoes. Would you agree to a proposal like this? If so, under what terms? If you are willing to join *their* affiliate program and put their link on your "Thank You" page, then word your proposal respectively. Show them the benefits they will get from it, quoting the average number of daily/monthly sales you get. Then explain that you are willing to do this if they also do this for you in return. If handled properly from the start, this recruitment method could be very beneficial for both parties.

Not Responding to Affiliate E-mails and Support Questions. One of the merchants that approached me with a proposal to manage his affiliate program made it explicit from the very start that he would fine me $10 for every unanswered affiliate query. This may seem rigid, but all affiliates would agree that it is just. The affiliate manager is there to provide *full* support for his/her affiliate program. Affiliates send you their questions for you to respond. They

140

turn to you for help. Do not turn away from them, or the next thing you'll see is them turning away from your affiliate program. Make it a rule to answer any affiliate e-mail (or query that comes in any other way) within 24 or 48 hours.

Bounce-backs from the Affiliate Manager E-mail Address. Make sure your affiliates never get those "recipient's disk quota exceeded", or any other similar failed e-mail delivery notifications.

Use of E-mail Addresses Based on Free Servers. Some affiliate managers may think about getting an e-mail address from a provider like Hotmail, Yahoo, Google (Gmail), or another free server. Some may think that it's safer for recruitment, others may just want a separate e-mail account for affiliate program management. Whatever your reasons may be, it is a *bad idea*. First of all, affiliates will not treat you seriously if you have a free e-mail address. Russians say: "When you meet a man, you judge him by his clothes; when you leave, you judge him by his heart." Your e-mail address is the "clothing" that they will look at first. Do not let it obstruct their way to knowing your heart with regards to affiliate marketing. Secondly, some spam filters will simply block your newsletters and promos if they have a combination of a free e-mail and a subject that looks suspicious.

If you can, get an @yourcompanyname.com e-mail address. These look much more professional and trustworthy. If you are OPM-ing, then a clientname@OPMcompany.com is a good way to do it.

Improper "From" Fields. When you set up your e-mail client, do not put "Affiliate Manager of <Company Name>" into the "From Name" field. Some affiliates' e-mail clients will get your long title cut off right at the "of" part, and affiliates will not be able to tell who the message came from, nor will they be able to find it in case they need it later on. Either use your own full name, and have the "Affiliate Manager of <Company Name>" in your signature in the body of the message; or fill your "From Name" field this way: "<Company Name>'s Affiliate Manager".

Similarly, flee from having "Affiliate Team" in your "From" label or message signature.

Lack of Communication. However obvious this is, I will stress it time and again: *talk* to your affiliates. No, I do not mean call them (many may not appreciate this close of attention), but communicate to them regularly. Notify them of any upcoming changes *in advance*. Ask for their feedback, and if it happens to be constructive, strive to make it a reality, and then announce any changes or improvements made on their request. Nitin Nohria, Professor of Business Administration at the Harvard Business School, said: "Communication is the real work of leadership". The affiliate manager is to be the motivational leader affiliates follow. Be one! Communicate enthusiastically, eloquently, soberly.

Informing Them of the Obvious. One of the biggest challenges of affiliate management is the fact that you, as the affiliate manager, have to market to the marketers. Be careful and selective with what you say and when you say it. Do not let your e-mails state the obvious. If your company makes its best sales during the Q4 season, remember that most everyone else's do, too. If you want to communicate that to your affiliates, communicate it to them differently. Quote the statistics: "During November-December our company makes 54% of the year's revenue." This would sound much better than, "Now is the time to push us, because it's our best sales time". Also, if they hear these Q4 stats from you a few months in advance, it is much better than informing them of this in the beginning of November. Calls like "Join us today, because now is the best sales time for us" may also not work as effectively as you wish. Even if they join you in October-November, there is little chance of them sending you considerable sales within a month or two of singing-up (unless they already have well-optimized sites for your product sitting on the shelf waiting for you – which is highly unlikely).

Ignoring Affiliate Suggestions. While the above point relates to your communication with affiliates, this one has to do with reacting to their suggestions. Let your affiliate program be a two-way street: not just you communicating to them, but also you acting in response to their propositions. Every suggestion you receive from an affiliate should be treated seriously, then replied to as such. Some affiliate managers take offense when affiliates point out errors to them. Do not ignore constructive criticism. With their help, you will be able to transform your program into the best affiliate program in your industry. Heed what they say and try to accommodate every reasonable proposition. Not every single proposition will be sound and/or feasible, but many will be. Do not repeat the mistakes of most affiliate networks, which, unfortunately, tend to ignore affiliate feedback. Be different! Be there for them, and it will eventually reflect in the sales they send you.

Low Quality Answers to Questions. When you are asked a specific question, give a specific answer. If you do not know the answer, dig into it, find it out, and then reply to your affiliate. It is a widely known fact that the best way to learn something is to teach someone else about it. When you receive questions you do not know the answers to, celebrate! They are *your* opportunities to grow.

You may also devote a part of your monthly newsletter to educating your affiliates on more advanced issues. These may include: working with datafeeds, parasites, optimizing your CTR in PPC bidding, as well as many other topics. You may fish them right out of the questions you get from your affiliates. Including such a section in your regular newsletter will make it an interesting read, not only for "newbie" affiliates, but also for the more advanced players of the affiliate game. It is obvious that most of the more advanced questions will require more than one paragraph, but do not overload your newsletter. Use the *educating paragraph* to give a brief introduction into the matter, as well as the benefits of this knowledge to affiliates, then give a link to an article on it. It is best that you compile the article yourself, as it will help to build you up in the eyes of the affiliates. If you are not able to write a full article on the question, you may always put together a creative, intriguing introduction, followed up by the major questions on the topic and the external hyperlinks to webpages that give the respective answers.

Asking Affiliates How they Can Do Better. Do not *ask them*, but propose your help to work shoulder-to-shoulder *with them* to bring their affiliate performance to the top level. Do not promise them what is not under your control, but ensure they know that you are willing to help.

Impersonality. Get personal with your affiliates. Find out their names and make sure they know yours. Find out when their birthdays are. These would be great days to present them with such sweet affiliate gifts as a 1 Week Two-Fold Commission Increase, or a Cash Bonus, or something of the kind. Do not alienate yourself from them by presenting

144

yourself as an XYZ.com's Affiliate Program Management Team, for example. It will not give you the desired respect and trust. The sequence is always in reverse: first you want to gain trust – not through impersonal presentation, but by works. Respect and mutual amiability will then naturally follow.

Newsletter Errors. These may be of two types: language mistakes (misspellings, improper grammar, incorrect URLs, etc) and code errors. Since the first type is self-explanatory, let me elaborate on the second one in more detail here. What do I imply by "code errors"? If your affiliate network or your in-house software has a function of "short codes" this is *wonderful*! Short codes may help you put together beautiful personalized newsletters, and I myself extensively use short codes in my correspondence with affiliates. However, beware of the risk they may carry. What I will say now may seem too basic for you, but trust me, errors like these discredit affiliate managers daily. Do not hand-type these short codes unless you really know what you are doing. I always recommend cutting and pasting to avoid e-mails that start with "Dear [affiliate_first_name]" – simply because you have forgotten to hit that "Shift" button to type in the proper {affiliate_first_name} short code. The legendary Willie Sutton wrote: "Success in any endeavor requires single-minded attention to detail and total concentration." Regardless of his occupation, I must agree.

Insisting on Trying to "Help". Do let your affiliates know that they can always count on your help with any questions pertaining to your affiliate program and their performance within it. Mention it in every newsletter you send out, but refrain from being pushy and too aggressive in your desire to help. Affiliates are in this business as much for the money they can earn from it, as for the freedom they have in it. Let them know they can count on you, but do not insist on your help when they are not specifically asking you for it. I have had situations when affiliates that performed wonderfully in one program I managed, showed miserable performance in another program. I knew that they could do much better than that, and I did approach them about it. However, instead of telling them I wanted to help them squeeze more out of the affiliate program in question, I offered them something they could not refuse – something that would motivate them enough to get out and DO it. The feedback was great; and I am quite positive I would not have not seen the same reaction had I simply written them a message on trying to help, then had sent an equally dry follow-up message in a week, followed by another one later. Be creative in how you approach them. Make it worth their time, and they will respond.

Total Unhelpfulness. There is another extreme to the above-mentioned "help" issue, and that is complete lack of helpfulness on the part of the merchant or the affiliate manager. When you are running an affiliate program – be it with or without an affiliate manager – affiliates will contact you with questions and requests for assistance. Do not leave those unattended; it will only demonstrate that you do not care about your program, and if you do not, why should they?

Selective Helping. This is yet another mistake connected with helping your affiliates. Some merchants and affiliate managers practice selective helping – communicating more willingly with their super-affiliates, and not as much with the "newbies". This is a serious error. I have had a "newbie" turn into the second best-performing affiliate within 5 months of sign-up! Divide your help and good-will equally amongst all your affiliates and watch yourself succeed in ways you never thought possible.

Insisting on Phoning. This was discussed briefly when touching on the methods of contacting your affiliates. In general, affiliates are very protective of their privacy and extremely defensive of their freedom. Insisting on calling them may have more of a negative effect on your relationship with them. Yes, do mention your contact telephone number(s) in every affiliate newsletter and every piece of outgoing e-mail, but do not insist on setting up a call of any kind unless they have initiated it.

Irrelevantly-Worded Newsletters. Do not simply type out the information you want to communicate. Your goal is to get it across and get it turned into sales. Remember the different affiliate groups and the different approaches each may require. If possible, e-mail different monthly newsletters to different groups of affiliates. By all means try to make your newsletter relevant, applicable, and motivating to do more for your program.

Improperly Formatted Newsletters. When putting together an affiliate newsletter, keep in mind *whom* you are writing it to and *what* you are writing it for. Your main goal should be to motivate your affiliates to do more for you. Achieve this by offering them practical help in the form of statistics, promos, examples of other affiliates' performances, ready-to-use links, banners and tracking codes. I have heard of merchants sending out affiliate newsletters that would, for the most part, contain only graphics, which is okay if you are writing to your customers. However, this is not appropriate for affiliate-geared newsletters, as these should be one of your main tools in regular affiliate communication, motivation, and implementation support.

Newsletters About the Future, While Excluding the Present. It is good to keep your affiliates informed of your plans. It is well-appreciated when you give them an idea of what you "have in stock" for them. But if you are planning on running an exciting Christmas promotion, and are announcing your plans around Thanksgiving time, I hope you have an equally exciting Thanksgiving promo to offer them a week or two before you make this announcement. The same applies to any changes within the program itself. If you have already changed something to the benefit of your affiliates, do announce it, and then briefly tell them of your future plans. But refrain from making grandiose future announcements if they do not yet know you as someone who will really do what is promised. Also, when you announce your future plans, always aim not just to satisfy their expectations, but to exceed them.

Treating Affiliates as Employees. See clause 15.1 in the sample Affiliate Program Agreement quoted at the very start of the Launch Phase questions and answers. It has been said that a perfect job is one that gives you the freedom to live your life the way you wish to live it. Keep in mind that affiliates are in this business exactly because of their appreciation of the freedom this work gives them. Flee from employee-worker associations in your e-mails and newsletters. Treat your affiliates like *business partners*. Respect their freedom, honor their devotion to your affiliate program, and they will appreciate it.

Termination of Affiliate Accounts Without Notice. While reviewing your affiliates' performance statistics, you may notice that a particular affiliate is sending you many clicks, but few, if any, sales. This may lead you to suspect such an affiliate of fraudulent behavior. Assumptions are fine; however, remember they are only *assumptions* unless proven to be fact. While you are looking into the clicks history, contact the affiliate directly. Talk to him/her. They may well be in need of your help with conversions, may feel frustrated about the situation, and may appreciate suggestions on how to improve their performance. Talk to them before you do anything, and *never* terminate an affiliate for inactivity or low performance.

Dryness & Blandness. Cultivate creativity. Being an affiliate manager implies motivating others (we will talk more about this in the last section of this book). If your communication and the whole creative inventory reflects a dry, bland and boring style, do not expect them to follow you. You are to be their source of enthusiasm and inspiration: let this be your mission if you really want them to sell for you. Keep in mind that many affiliates get dozens of private offers on a daily basis from other affiliate programs. Some of these propositions may well be your competitors'. Make your affiliate management style stand out – through contests, commission increase offers, bonuses, large end-of-year prizes to the best performers, professionally created banners and readiness to custom-make banners of virtually any size for individual affiliates, etc, etc – and you will be listened to.

Unkept Promises. When you promise your affiliates something, keep your word. If you have to, write everything down to remember what was promised to which affiliate, and exactly when it was promised. If you do not follow your words up with actions, the automatic conclusion will be that you are an affiliate manager/program that does not keep promises. Word like this can spread like wildfire, and your reputation could go up in smoke.

Ultimatums. Some merchants may word their affiliate correspondence in such a way that their e-mail messages sound like ultimatums, containing demands (as opposed to suggestions) for activation or sales of a particular number or monetary amount. This most certainly is not a display of professionalism. In fact, it will only reveal your amateurship and desperation. Do not demand from your affiliates, say, to produce at least one sale within the next month, threatening to remove them from your affiliate program. This will *not* motivate them, but it will most certainly do you a disservice. Not only will these affiliates drop your program before you even think of analyzing their end-of-month statistics, but they will also let others know of such practices, harming both your own reputation and the reputation of your affiliate program.

Insisting on Homepage Links. Links on the affiliate's homepage may or may not get you some good traffic. If/when an affiliate suggests a different page within their website for your link(s), carefully consider their reasoning. Their homepage may not always be a good place for your ad to show. Your goal is to have your links on webpages with intense and highly-targeted traffic. At times, this may mean pages other than the homepage.

Insisting on Promotion of Bestsellers. Do inform your affiliates of your bestsellers and create respective banners, text links, or other ways for them to feature these bestsellers. However, do not insist that they promote them. Some affiliates may not want to focus on the bestsellers, because other affiliates are already pushing them actively. Some affiliates would rather go with the other items you sell, and

150

that is absolutely fine. Affiliates often know best what fits their websites better. Offer your help, but do it gently.

Lack of Advance Notifications. Be it seasonal promotions, coupons, or any other announcements and/or enhancements to your affiliate program, give your affiliates enough time to prepare for the changes. At the time you become aware of these, give your affiliates the courtesy of also letting them know. With promotions, send out one advance announcement, describing it about 10 days before the promo. Then, send another one a few days before the promo begins. Not all affiliates have the capability to set dates in their databases. Notify them duly.

Showing An Affiliate's Site to Others. Never do this without getting prior approval from the affiliate whose website's URL you want share with another affiliate(s). Remember that affiliates compete with each other, and as it is in any competition, there are a lot of unethical practices involved, one of these being site copying. Unless you have received the affiliate's "go ahead" on sharing his/her website's information with another affiliate, do not do this.

Changes that Affect Affiliate Links. If you delete a product from your website, either keep the affiliate thumbnail image on your server, or have it replaced with a default "Sold Out" image. This way the websites of your datafeed affiliates will not have "broken images" until they update the datafeed. The same advice applies to all other changes within the merchant website that may affect affiliate websites. Things that may seem small to the merchant (like changing the size of your thumbnail images from 120x120 to 100x100, or rounding up the prices from .95 to .00), will cause a major headache for your affiliates. If you persistently make changes that affect thousands of their links, and fail to notify them of these changes in advance, they will drop your program sooner than later. If things like these are not under your control as an affiliate manager, let your employer read this paragraph, stressing the importance of the point in question

Customer-Geared Newsletters. Unless your affiliates specifically request it, do not sign them up for the customer-geared newsletters. Communicate with them via affiliate newsletters. Most of them are in this business to *sell* for you, not to *buy* from you.

Late Payments. No excuses. "We can't pay you until they pay us" is never an excuse to withhold payment from your affiliates. This always reminds me of the way salaries were, and still are, paid in the former Soviet Union: people would work for months without pay, not getting their January paycheck until July. No "Soviet Union excuses" in affiliate marketing, please!

Part 3
Ideas for
Affiliate Program Promotion

If you have an apple and I have an apple and we exchange these apples, then you and I still each have one apple. But if you have an idea and I have an idea and we exchange these ideas, then each of us will have two ideas.

George Bernard Shaw

George Bernard Shaw put this in the best possible way. I am a strong believer in sharing ideas. Ideas, in all their intangibility, are what move marketing. Ideas unleashed into the world change the world. The best ideas turn into ideaviruses (thanks to Seth Godin for a beautiful book on this!), the good ideas turn your own work, and the work of those under your guidance, into fun. An affiliate once told me how much she appreciates the component of fun in the promotions I run for the affiliate programs I manage. She said, "If I can't have the fun, I don't want to play". Ideally, your whole management work should be saturated by a subconscious strive to turn everyone's routine tasks into work that is pleasurable. Do not underestimate the power of fun. Speaking from experience, I can testify that when your affiliate management style is undergirded by original, out-of-the-box thinking, this makes life fun, and you'll be on the road to success.

How does one cultivate the idea-generating spirit? You may be reading these lines thinking, "This is just not me. I am not an idea generator. I have no talent for this." And you may be right. Neuroscientific concepts on brain lateralization applied to marketing tell us that most marketers are either right brain or left brain dominant. The right-brainers are best fit for creative work, while the left-brainers are better at performing analytical tasks. Combinations of both in one individual are rare, or even extraordinary. Now, turning to the comments of those that struggle with creativity in marketing - those left-brain marketers of the affiliate world- let me tell you: do not despair! Learn from the ideas of others, modify them to fit your context, synergize them with your own thoughts, then polish and tailor them to work for your specific needs. Remember the words of the wise Irish dramatist, and take it even further – take my idea, couple it with yours, and produce a third one that becomes a synergy

155

of the two. Keep exercising in idea breeding regularly and you will inevitably succeed.

My ideas are no secret. I believe in growing the affiliate marketing industry by sharing ideas – posting them Internet-wide at various message boards and forums. What follows has been put together for you to use. Yes, you've heard me right: be my guest! Use them, transform them, customize them. Make your affiliates' life fun and the avenues of their gratefulness paved with affiliate sales will be endless.

The ideas I bring to your attention below are not arranged in any specific order. Many of them are totally unique, while others are inspired by marketers working in industries other than affiliate marketing. Yet others are modified versions of what I have seen other affiliate managers using. I hope they will help you in the management of your own affiliate program.

Idea #1 – *Better Base Conditions for Select Affiliates*

This was one of the first ideas I had when I started managing affiliate programs: offer better base conditions for select groups of affiliates. They could be affiliates that belong to a particular forum or an online community. Let's say the base commission of your affiliate program is 10% and it has the cookie life set at 90 days. Offer 12% instead of the 10%, and/or 120 days of cookie life to those affiliates that sign up to your program through a specific link, online forum, or during a set period of time from the official launch date of the program. You may not only play with the commission rate and the cookie days, but also offer particular monetary per-sale bonuses. These bonuses may be lifetime or time-restricted. Commission and cookie life increases are always to be for life.

<u>Hint</u>: Taking this idea further, you may apply it to private offers sent to those affiliates that you know link to your competition (see the sample recruitment e-mail in the Questions & Answers section).

Idea #2 – *Free Domain Giveaway*

Everyone loves gifts. Those affiliates that are at the dawn of their affiliate marketing path appreciate them more than anyone. Contests are motivational and productive, all at once. Merchants are often much better equipped to come up with effective domain name ideas. Come up with a few domain names fitting your merchant's product(s) better, and then register them. If you are having a hard time coming up with the names, ask the company's management or their marketing team for help/ideas. Domain names should be picked with a goal in mind, and your ultimate goal is to have affiliates use them for the websites that would send you sales. Once you have registered these domains, announce a Free Domain Giveaway where you will be transferring the ownership of the domains to those affiliates that have performed a particular action (examples: joining your program by a set date; putting together a comprehensive datafeed-based website featuring all of your products on it; or else incorporating your affiliate program's banners, links, product pictures, links or descriptions into the content of their website).

Depending on what your affiliate program promotes, you may choose to classify the domains you give away into different categories. For example, a cosmetics affiliate program's manager may think up and register domains fit for data feed-based sites that sell only the merchant's cosmetics, as well as domain names for content-based websites. These websites, may, for example, be devoted to articles on skin care and the like, and also allow your affiliate to promote your products and/or links on the side.

Advice: Make sure you state all restrictions in the conditions of the giveaway, or you may end up having an affiliate promote your competitors' products side-by-side yours on the domain name you have purchased!

Idea #3 – *Arithmetic Progression Bonuses*

The way of remunerating your affiliates using this method is not new. You pay bonuses on every sale. The pattern of calculating bonuses, on the other hand, is one that I have never seen used by other affiliate managers. This pattern is based on an arithmetic progression. You set the common difference and then increase each new bonus by that difference. For example: if your common difference is 5 and you are willing to pay a $10 bonus with the first sale, the second sale bonus would then be $15, while the third sale bonus would be $20, and so on.

As any "per every sale" bonus method, this one would work best for newly launched programs, as well as for programs that are in need of revitalizing.

Advice: Ensure that the conditions of such a bonus campaign clearly lists the time period during which the bonuses will be paid out. Also, do your math and preliminary research (you could really use those left-brain marketers here) so as not to run bankrupt as a result of the campaign.

Idea #4– *Co-Branded Version of a Good Affiliate Tool*

There are plenty of useful affiliate tools, such as software applications, scripts, and the like, that make affiliate life easier, helping to promote your products more efficiently. One of them has been put together by the CEO of the Fourth

World Media Corporation, a talented software developer and a good friend, Richard Gaskin. The piece of software I am referring to is, of course, the world-famous WebMerge.

The idea that came to my mind in October of 2005 is one of which I am particularly proud, and I will tell you the reason why shortly. First of all, let us look into what we did with Richard. I had approached him that Fall with an idea of making a custom version of WebMerge to fit a particular data feed. WebMerge is a wonderful universal tool, excellent for integrating most any affiliate program's data feed into the affiliate website. However, there are at least two reasons an affiliate thinks twice before ordering it from the Fourth World. First of all, affiliates have to do their homework before they can really utilize the software with data feeds from various merchants. Secondly, the cost of the software – however modest it is – may be deemed as a substantial investment by some. The idea was to make it both more affordable and more applicable. The result was the co-branded special edition of WebMerge – "WebMerge RL: Russian Legacy Edition". It turned out to be over 55% less expensive than the full version ($44.00 instead of $99.00), and it still allowed room for the upgrade to the full version if the affiliate felt comfortable using it with the Russian Legacy's data feed. This unique software piece is still available at www.fourthworld.com/products/webmerge/rl.html, and you are more than welcome to try it yourself.

I have mentioned that I take a special pride in this idea. Let me tell you why. Ten months after the launch of the WebMerge RL, the ShareASale affiliate network launched the "WebMerge: ShareASale Special Edition".

Idea #5 – *Segment Your Products*

It is no secret that many affiliates like to "specialize", or work in particular verticals and build websites on a select number of topics. Let's say one likes children and promotes only sites related to babies, parenting, and education, for example. Another may have a few websites with good "Home & Garden" traffic, and this affiliate, of course, would be great for selling kitchen, garden, and home-related merchandise. The list could go on, but my point is the following: if the merchant whose affiliate program you promote carries an inventory that allows you to segment it by products related to various topics, do set aside some time to do the segmentation. You will then be able to offer your affiliates some nice practical advice on how to market those specific groups of products at their websites. Such segmentation works wonderfully for merchants selling collectibles, memorabilia, books, magazines, etc. Once you have performed the segmentation and grouping of products into topical categories, project the results of your research to the affiliates, telling them how they can use this information. Such homework of yours will tell your affiliates you really care. When they see you treat them with understanding and show them your sincere desire for their success, they will respond accordingly.

Idea #6 – *Learn to Celebrate*

Celebrate everything with your affiliates. Put together a calendar of dates important to the company that is running an affiliate program, and celebrate these dates with your affiliates. Good examples of such dates would be: the date when the company was established (call it" Our Company's Birthday"), the date when the affiliate program was started (you may call it" Affiliate Program's Birthday"), or the date when a particular long-term promotion or bonus type was introduced into the life of your affiliates.

If you sell ink, dig into the history and you will find out that ink was developed by the Chinese some 5000 year ago. They used it for blackening the raised surfaces of pictures and texts they carved in stone. What a beautiful picture to precede your next promotion campaign that could elaborate on the number 5000. As an example, 5000 may be used to translate into 100 bonuses $50 each to add-up into the total prize fund of $5000. You may give these bonuses for every batch of $500 in sales that an affiliate sends you. Announce it to your affiliates and then sweeten the deal by clarifying that this promo is *non*-exclusive of all and/or any other promos run by our program!! The number of $50.00 checks to be given away is exactly 100, and this promotion campaign is not limited by time (i.e.: it is to be run until the last check is given out). In addition, the number of bonuses to be given out per affiliate is also *un*limited. The number of $50.00 checks an affiliate may receive is tied only to the number of $500 batches of sales they send to you. This has been tried and proven effective. Use it confidently. If your number isn't as large as 5000, and you have to base your campaign on a number 154 – that is fine, too. Staying with the ink affiliate program example, you can give out 154 ink cartridges to all affiliates that show you a 154% sales growth within the next month. The numbers do not have to be round for you to use them effectively. Any anniversary is just a reason for you to make the life of your affiliates more fun. Motivate them to do more for your affiliate program in a fun way and they will appreciate it.

If you are an outsourced affiliate manager, running several affiliate programs and posting around various affiliate forums, celebrate every round number of posts reached by you on any given forum. Let's say you've reached your 500th post. Run a cross-program promotion with a common prize fund of $500 (see one described below under Cross-Program Promotions).

Hint: If you run your ideas by your merchants first, you will be surprised how many of them will be supportive (both emotionally, and financially) of such promos. If you are an outsourced program manager, be prepared that sometimes you will have to invest your own funds into campaigns like the ones quoted under this idea. However, do remember to run the idea by the merchant first. It may save you a buck or two that you will be able to invest into affiliate recruitment, for example.

Idea #7 – *Run "Happy Weeks"*

The "Happy Weeks" idea came to me while thinking again over the Happy Meal™ concept pioneered by the McDonald's Corporation back in 1979. For close to 30 years the idea has been working well for its developers. Renowned motivational speaker Warren Greshes – the author of a premier audio/video program "Supercharged Selling: The Power to Be the Best"– while speaking at a convention, once referred to the Happy Meal™ concept by stating:

> "Kids wanted the toy... Kids wanted the box. You know why? Because kids don't buy food. They buy fun. They figure they can get food anywhere.
> What is your Happy Meal? What is it that you're willing to do for all your customers, your clients, your prospects that no one else is willing to do? How are you differentiating yourself from the competition?"

You know my stand on the component of fun in marketing. So it occurred to me one day that since none of us really ever fully grows up, we could all use a little extra happiness every

162

week, and my affiliates are no exception. I then started running "Happy Weeks" for all of the affiliate programs I managed. Each "Happy Week" was meant to be different, joyous, and incorporate fresh ideas of affiliate motivation. It was a challenging task, but it definitely paid off. Since the idea of "Happy Weeks" is more of a concept, a promotional framework, or even a philosophy, if you will, it may encompass any or all of the above and below-quoted ideas.

Idea #8 – *Classic "Happy Week" Idea*

This idea will probably work best for the very first Happy Week you run for your affiliate program – each day of the working week (read: Monday through Friday) should be attached to one letter in the word HAPPY:

Monday - **H**
Tuesday - **A**
Wednesday - **P**
Thursday - **P**
Friday - **Y**

Then let the focus of each day correspond to the letter that is attached to it. Here is how we did it for FantasyJewelryBox.com:

> "H" for **Homework** – The following question was asked: Did you know that there is a characteristic by which Cubic Zirconia simulated diamonds actually prevail over natural diamonds? Which one is it? Prizes were given away. The correct answer was: CZ contains more fire (or flashes of rainbow colors) than natural diamonds.
> "A" for **Ambition** – A Merriam-Webster Dictionary definition of "ambition" was quoted: "an ardent desire for…", "a desire to achieve a particular end". The printscreens of affiliate statistics were presented. They testified for a great conversion of the

affiliate program for a particular type of affiliates – coupon sites. Affiliates (especially the coupon ones) were motivated to work closer with the program.

"**P**" for **Prize** – Generate 5 sales within the next 24 hours, and I will credit your affiliate account $50! The program was still very new, and we had to run promos like this to motivate affiliates to be more aggressive.

"**P**" for **Prize** again – As expected, only one affiliate has come close to the goal, but not close enough to reach it. So we simplified the requirements, calling for 4 sales within 24 hours for the same prize of $50.

"**Y**" for **Your Chance** – The following call for action was posted on Friday morning: "Put up our links and send $150+ in sales by the end of the weekend, and I will credit your affiliate account a $20.00 bonus on top of your regular commission."

In another affiliate program's Happy Week promo, we used the first "P" for *Potential*, while the second one for *Proliferated Commission*. On the Potential Day we asked affiliates to look through our inventory and guess what product category has the best selling potential. On the second "P" Day we promised them that whoever sends in two or more sales within the next 24 hours would get a *two*-fold commission increase for the rest of the month. It was posted on the 15th of the month, so the offer was still quite attractive.

Idea #9 – *An A-B-C-D-E Idea*

The very first Happy Week we ran for RussianLegacy.com had each day of the working week follow a letter of the Latin alphabet:

1st Day - Monday - **A**
2nd Day - Tuesday - **B**
3rd Day - Wednesday - **C**

4th Day - Thursday - **D**
5th Day - Friday - **E**

Each letter of the alphabet attached to the day of the week stood for the way that particular day was named. For example:

"**A**" – **Adjustment(s) Day** – the day when we asked affiliates for their feedback on our affiliate program, calling on them for advice on adjustments that would to help us make the program better.

"**B**" – **Bonus Day** – the day when we promised each affiliate a $20.00 bonus on all $150+ sales generated during that day. Each time the bonus was awarded, we provided affiliates with the printscreens of those affiliate transactions. Nothing inspires better than picturesque testimonials.

"**C**" – **Coupon Day** – the day when we announced the Coupon of the Week (its expiration date was set exactly a week after the date it was posted), making it a substantial discount coupon on an expensive category of items on which we had a nice profit margin.

"**D**" – **Domain Day** – the day that we used for the announced two domain names to be given away: SovietGift.com and RussianGiftBasket.com. These domains had to be used for quality datafeed-based websites, but the domain giveaway was not limited only to Thursday; Thursday was just the day we used to announce the giveaway.

"**E**" – **Easy Cash** – announcement was made that everyone who generates a cumulative value of $400 or larger in affiliate sales from Friday through Sunday would get a $100 check on top of their regular commission. As sales volumes naturally drop down on weekends, this campaign was meant to motivate better affiliate promotion activity during the weekend.

The A-B-C-D-E idea may, of course, be used for other time periods: each week of the month, or each month of the year. The concept is easy to follow, and affiliates openly admitted that they were looking forward to learning what the next letter of the alphabet would stand for. It adds an element of intrigue to the promo, capturing the affiliate attention and keeping them interested until the end of the campaign.

Idea #10 – A 1-2-3-4-5 Idea

This idea is very similar to the above one, with the only difference that each day of the working week is tied to a number reflecting the order each work day occupies in the week:

> 1st Day - Monday - **number 1**
> 2nd Day - Tuesday - **number 2**
> 3rd Day - Wednesday - **number 3**
> 4th Day - Thursday - **number 4**
> 5th Day - Friday - **number 5**

I will give you two examples of how you can use the numbers. We ran our 1-2-4-4-5 Happy Weeks for two programs simultaneously: one for the RussianLegacy.com, while the other one for FantasyJewelryBox.com. These campaigns were not only run at the same time, but also at the same place (at a popular affiliate marketing forum). So I had to use my imagination to keep the promos different for each of the affiliate programs. Here is what I did:

FantasyJewelryBox's 1-2-3-4-5 Happy Week

"1" for **1 Affiliate that…** – …generates the most sales at FJB between now and the end of this month will receive an additional $10.00 Performance Bonus. This was announced on a Monday that happened to be the 29th day of a 31-day month.
"2" for **2 Announcements** – this day was used to announce two coming enhancements to the client's affiliate program.
"3" for **3 Levels of Commission Increase** – announced that starting from that moment and until the end of the next month

we would be paying affiliates increased commissions on larger gross monthly sales sent to us.

"4" for **the First 4 Affiliates that...** – ...reach a threshold of $1000 in the current month will get a $50 Bounty on top of their commission. This is in addition to the *already increased* commission announced the day before.

"5" for **5 $10 Bills to 5 Active Affiliates** – announcement was made that the first 5 affiliates that show a 5 times growth in the current month over the previous month will receive a $50 prize check each.

RussianLegacy's 1-2-3-4-5 Happy Week

"1" for **1 Huge Discount/Coupon** – announced an affiliate-exclusive coupon giving a $200 discount on one particular item. This offer had two main advantages to affiliates: (i) the coupon was not available to customers in any other way but through affiliate websites, (ii) even with such a large discount, the affiliate commission on this item amounted to almost $50.

"2" for **2 Good News** – on Tuesday we published the news on two important improvements to the program that affiliates had themselves asked for.

"3" for **a "3 Color" Contest** – ran a contest on the best affiliate idea on how to promote Russian Legacy's products in an original way, utilizing the three colors of the Russian flag. Prize: choice of RL's merchandise ranging from $25 to $31 in price.

"4" for **the First 4 Affiliates that...** – same idea as the one quoted above in the FJB's Week.

"5" for **Every 5th Sale Bonus** – special $50 bonus was announced to be awarded on every 5th sale during the current month.

Once again, just as with the A-B-C-D-E idea, the 1-2-3-4-5 principle would also be a wonderful fit for either the four weeks of the month, or the twelve months of the year.

Idea #11 – *Sliding Scale of Commission Increases*

Since I have already somewhat touched upon this idea in the framework of the 1-2-3-4-5 Week we ran for FJB, let me elaborate on this in a separate paragraph. I believe this idea deserves special attention, as it fits best into periods much longer than a day or a week. This idea may be used well within a period of one month, half a year, or even a year. The idea is simple: you offer your affiliates higher commission levels on larger sales sent to you. The commission increases they get kick in with a fairly small amount of sales sent in – something achievable and realistic. Affiliates – especially those that send you zero hits/sales – do not get motivated by promos calling on them to "generate $5000 in sales during the next month". Look at it from their point of view. Provide testimonials demonstrating the achievability of the task (if possible, backed up with printscreens that have affiliate names and details blanked out, of course), and make it attractive and motivating.

If you have started running a program for a merchant with a large profit margin (examples: inexpensive jewelry, certain publications, etc), talk to the owners of the business, or whoever overseas the affiliate program management, and offer them a sliding scale of commission increases as a promo that could jump-start the program. I had a merchant with the base commission set at 10% that agreed to cut his own profit for the sake of jump-starting his program. So we ran the following one-month campaign:

- Send a total of $500 in sales – get a 15% commission on all of them
- Send $1000 in sales – get 20% in commissions
- Send $2000 in sales – get 25% commission on all of them

A month down the road when the sales did pick up, but we remembered the success of the above-quoted offer, we raised some of the qualifying amounts, also offering more attractive commission increases:

- Send a total of $500 in sales – get a 20% commission on all of them
- Send $1500 in sales – get 25% in commissions
- Send $2699+ in sales – get 30% commission on all of them

We were basically offering a 200% increase of the default 10% commission if they reach $500 in sales, a 250% increase for $1500, and a 300% increase for $2699+ in sales.

I am convinced that one way or another, the above-described commission increase idea will work for *any* affiliate program. Be prepared, however, that some merchants may consider the above as additional expenses – expenses they "didn't expect". One merchant (with whom I was negotiating while discussing the possibility of taking on the management of his affiliate program), even called this commission increase idea "hidden charges". That was the last time we talked. Be prepared that you may need to open the merchant's eyes to the fact that any marketing is always an investment, and not just an expense article on their balance sheet. Be ready to show the advantages of running a flexible, performance-rewarding affiliate program, one that respects its affiliates and knows how to show it.

Idea #12 – *Colors Idea*

Along with numbers and letters of the alphabet, you may use colors (for example, colors of the rainbow) in your affiliate promos. The number of the colors in the rainbow matches the number of the days in the week. I find this very convenient. Each color has a meaning. Play with the symbolism of color, and make another week, month, or year in the life of your affiliates' a little more fun. Here is an example of a color-based campaign that we ran for one of the merchants (it lasted one working week):

Summary:

1st Day - Monday - **Red**
2nd Day - Tuesday - **Orange**
3rd Day - Wednesday - **Yellow**
4th Day - Thursday - **Green**
5th Day - Friday - **Blue**

Details:

Red Color... - the color of energy, war, danger, strength, power, determination, passion, desire, and love. We focused on power, determination, passion and desire. They are obviously the characteristics of those affiliates than any affiliate manager enjoys working with the most. What we did was an offer of 90 days to 365 days cookie life increase + a $5.00 bonus to all those that put together a nice datafeed-based website (at least two-thirds of the datafeed had to be used) within 10 days of the announcement.
Orange Color... - known as the color of enthusiasm, fascination, happiness, creativity, determination, attraction, success, encouragement, and stimulation. Hence, Tuesday was our Encouragement/Stimulation Day when we showed everyone a printscreen of the best program's affiliate (keeping his name and website address secret, of course), seeking to motivate others by his impressive statistics.
Yellow Color... - the color of sunshine, the color that's associated with joy, happiness, intellect, and energy. We used this day to show everyone a product we had in yellow colors, introducing a whole line of products affiliates often overlooked; but with the nice meanings the yellow color has, you may certainly use it differently.

Green Color... - the color of nature. It symbolizes growth, harmony, freshness, and fertility. Green has a strong emotional correspondence with safety. Dark green is also commonly associated with money. What better chance to stress the main idea of the week: to get as many people as possible to start using our datafeed. I told affiliates that I would throw in $50+ worth of the merchant's products as a prize for all those that integrate our datafeed into their sites within 16 hours of this announcement (and this was to happen *on top* of the already-promised cookie life increase to 365 days and the $5.00 bonus). **Blue Color...** - the color of the sky and sea. It is often associated with depth and stability. Interestingly enough, dark blue - associated with depth, expertise, and stability - is a preferred color for corporate America. So I focused on *stability*, and announced to all affiliates that the merchant is officially going free of 4th click on GoldenCAN, letting them own 100% of their traffic and sales.

As mentioned at the onset, you may also use the remaining two colors of the **Indigo** and **Violet** for Saturday and Sunday. *Indigo* symbolizes intuition, meditation, deep contemplation, while *violet* stands for interchange or unity. Both colors' meanings are excellent for tying them up with a weekend analysis of your program, and coming up with suggestions for improvements.

<u>Variation</u>: If it suits your affiliate program, you may also use the meanings of different flowers (this would work wonderfully for flower-sending merchants), picking up 5 or 7 for the week, 12 for twelve months of the year, or 28-31 for the days in the month.

Idea #13 – *Lingua-Symbolic Idea for One Week*

Being a professional linguist, I have always been fascinated by correlations between the meaning of words and their origin. I was brought up in a country that speaks a Romance language, being born and raised in Chişinău,

Moldova, where Romanian is the language of the state. Years before even thinking of studying linguistics professionally, I had noticed that the name of each day of the week is tied to a name of a planet. Monday is "luni" in Romanian, and "Luna" is the Moon, for example. Tuesday is "miercuri", which of course, relates to Mercury.

Later on, in the university classroom (I hold a B.A. and an M.A. in Linguistics), I found out that the seven-day system we now use is based on an ancient astrological notion – that the seven known celestial bodies influence what happens on Earth, and that each of these celestial bodies controls the first hour of the day named after it. This system was brought into Hellenistic Egypt from Mesopotamia, where astrology had been practiced for millennia and where seven had always been a propitious number. In A.D. 321, the Emperor Constantine the Great grafted this astrological system onto the Roman calendar. He made the first day of this new week a day of rest and worship for all, and imposed the following sequence and names to the days of the week. This new Roman system was adopted with modifications throughout most of Western Europe:

Celestial Body	LATIN	ENGLISH	ITALIAN	FRENCH
Sun	Solis	Sunday	domenica	dimanche
Moon	Lunae	Monday	lunedì	lundi
Mars	Martis	Tuesday	martedì	mardi
Mercury	Mercurii	Wednesday	mercoledì	mercredi
Jupiter	Jovis	Thursday	giovedì	jeudi
Venus	Veneris	Friday	venerdì	vendredi
Saturn	Saturni	Saturday	sabato	samedi

As you might have already guessed, the Happy Week was based on the names and meanings of planets corresponding to days from Monday (lunedì) through Friday (venerdì), and it went like this:

Monday - **Moon Day** - If there were one day that the affiliate marketing world proclaimed the day of the industry, it would probably have been Monday. So many of us in this industry are true "children of the moon" (coding under the moonlight until 3 or 4 am, getting our best inspiration for sites' promotion, PPC methods, content associations and affiliate promo campaigns, all by the light of the stars). The basic planetary association connected with the moon has to do with *reacting to something*. My call was as simple as 1-2-3: put up 1 link by Tuesday, send 2 sales by Friday, and get a 3-fold commission increase on all sales this week. We had a winner before I posted the next day's post.

Tuesday - **Mars Day** - Mars is traditionally associated with asserting, *making things happen*, express positively, fighting for (especially beliefs). I called affiliates to "make things happen" – join our affiliate program, put up links and receive the $10 activation bonus that was advertised in the welcoming e-mail.

Wednesday - **Mercury Day** - Mercury is often called the *communication* planet. So we had a Communication Wednesday, when I communicated to affiliates what problems had been resolved and what new features had been introduced to the program since the last week.

Thursday - **Jupiter Day** - Jupiter is traditionally associated with maturing, *developing* and *growing*. To motivate everyone to develop and grow in the capacity of FJB affiliate, I made a special deal for all affiliates that had generated 0 sales before that day: I committed to pay them doubled commissions on all sales generated between that Thursday and the beginning of the next week.

Friday - **Venus Day** - Venus is connected with *marking as different*; valuing. I communicated to my affiliates that I wanted to single out one affiliate – the one that generated sales for the highest total amount by the end of Sunday (by 11:59 PST). That affiliate was promised to be "valued" and "marked as different", by getting a $20 bonus payment into their affiliate account.

As with all other ideas, feel free to modify this one to fit your own situation and goals.

Idea #14 – *Bonus Weeks*

Besides offering performance bonuses to affiliates that reach particular goals within one month, one quarter, or one year, remember to run bonus weeks. They do work well, but the conditions of bonus weeks have to look extremely attractive. Affiliates must be motivated enough to set everything else aside and start putting up the links to your program and your coupons, or start setting up PPC campaigns, leading traffic to you. If you can afford to give away $100 for $499.99+ in weekly sales, this would be a very nice incentive. If you can't, see if you can afford to live with a $50 bonus for $399.99+ in weekly sales, and $100 bonus for $699.99+ in sales, or something similar. Talk to the merchant and try to make the bonus as attractive for the "end user" (your affiliate) as possible, yet do not undercut the merchant's profit so much that it turns the affiliate program into an unprofitable venture.

Idea #15 – *Growth Tied to Commission*

Do not concentrate on giving away only money. Many affiliates would much prefer a commission increase to the money. So, since your ultimate goal is your program's growth, why not stimulate that growth by offering higher commissions to those that show they can have an impact on it. Run a campaign like this one: Every affiliate that shows you a 2-fold growth in weekly sales (compared to your weekly average and based on the last 8 weeks' performance) this week/month, will get a 2-fold commission increase for the

174

whole of the next month. You may also throw in a $10 cash bonus for everyone who reaches the 2-fold growth goal. Set the exact deadline when this offer expires and when you will analyze the outcome of the promo. When/if you have any winners, congratulate them openly (through newsletters and forums). Testimonials of other people's successes can be a great form of encouragement.

Idea #16 – *Offer Tripled Commission*

This may sound unreal to some merchants, but if you are not offering a 25+% commission to your affiliates, why not run a tripled commission campaign once in a while? Although you may make it as short as a 3 day campaign, I would not recommend anything shorter than one week. You may offer the tripled commission in the following cases:

- To affiliates that show you the growth that justifies the campaign (you will need to sit down with the merchant to agree on the calculations)
- To all affiliates on all sales of $XXX.XX or larger
- On select products to which you want your affiliates' attention drawn

Again, when you have winners, make sure you share their achievements and awards with others. I had an affiliate earning 36% commissions on the program with a default commission of 12%. However, since she was earning it on items that the company made over 55% on, the merchant didn't mind.

You may certainly also run double commission promotions, and attach cash bonuses to whatever pattern you decide to go with. If you do a double commission promo, it

175

may be a good idea to tie that to a double increase in sales over a particular period of time. For example:

> "Every affiliate that shows a two-fold growth in weekly sales (compared to your weekly average and based on the last 8 weeks' performance), in the course of any week during the following four weeks, will get a two-fold commission increase on all sales generated during that week (a "Happy" one for you, to be sure!). *And* to make your life even sweeter, I will also throw in a $20.00 cash bonus into every affiliate account that shows me the growth by next Monday."

The above should be communicated to affiliates on Monday to give them one full week to work on trying to increase their sales two-fold, aiming at getting not only the commission increase, but also the cash bonus. The period during which you run this promo may be of any length: 5 weeks, 6 weeks, etc.   Make sure you let them know if you are willing to reward *every* week that they show the growth, and if so, how the growth will be calculated (i.e.: comparing to what weeks). Do not make it overly complicated though.   Word it clearly and attractively. If needed, use bullet points.

Play with the general concept of tripled or doubled commissions to generate your own variations. Be creative; make the work pleasurable and the goal rewarding.

Idea #17 – *Run a Lottery*

There are two ways to communicate the largest sale amounts within your program to your affiliates: (i) tell them the numbers up-front, or (ii) tell them the numbers up-front, but in such a form that will make them remember these numbers, or at least the ranges of numbers. In the beginning of October 2006, I came up with an idea of running a lottery. I picked out the five largest amounts of sales that occurred within one affiliate program over the period of ten days, and invited my affiliates to take part in the following contest:

> During the period of the last 10 days our affiliate program has seen XXX sales. Some of them were too beautiful not to quote, but instead of simply showing you the numbers and the commissions paid out, I thought it would be nice to do it the fun way. Let's have a lottery!
>
> Here are the amounts of the top 5 sales:
>
> $178.55
> $188.64
> $244.95
> $315.34
> $340.45
>
> <u>Task</u>: Kindly put them into the correct chronological order
>
> <u>Condition</u>: One guess taken from each affiliate.
>
> <u>Prize</u>: $50.00 sent to *each* winner via PayPal (you will be sent $52.50 so that the PayPal commission charges are covered by us)
>
> <u>Deadline</u>: Monday, 9 October, 10:08 AM EST
>
> The lottery will be run for one full work week. I am looking forward to your guesses. Remember, the number of $50.00 bills to be given out is *un*limited.

To find out how many possible variations of 5 entry sequences there could be, we need to find the factorial of 5. The *factorial* of a number is *the product of all the whole numbers, except zero, that are less than or equal to that number*. To find the factorial of 5 you would multiply together all the whole numbers, except zero, that are less than or equal to 5. Like this:

5 x 4 x 3 x 2 x 1 = 120

Hence, there were 120 different ways of answering the question posed in our contest. This secured us well enough, yet gave every participant a realistic enough of a chance to win the prize. In the above-quoted lottery we had 7 participants, and only one came close to the actual sequence, guessing:

$315.34
$178.55
$244.95
$340.45
$188.64

However, unfortunately for the participant, the last two had to be swapped for him to earn his $50 prize. We had no winners.

Theoretically, you may run a lottery based on 12 numbers. However, considering that the total number of possible sequences is over 479 million, I would not recommend it, regardless of how large a prize you offer. A lottery based on 7 numbers with a large prize would probably be the largest I would run. The factorial of 7 is 5,040.

Idea #18 – *Let Them "Test-Drive" It*

If you are selling a product/service that may be used by affiliates, let them "test-drive" it. If it is multi-domain hosting, you do not have to offer affiliates full ten or twenty-domain packages, but can create a custom affiliate package with hosting capability of two or three full domains. If it is gum, send them a sample to try once they send in their first or second sale. If it is coffee, send them coffee. If you are printing business cards, print a certain quantity for each affiliate free of charge. And you do not have to do any of these "test-driving" promotions just for the sake of the "test-driving" itself. In fact, I believe that they should *never* be detached from your ultimate goal – to get your affiliate program to generate sales. When you are giving anything away for free, there is a very big chance that the giveaway will diminish the value of what is given away. It may also lead some to assume that the quality of what is being given away is not as high if it is free. This latter possibility will hopefully be waived once they actually try it (again, I am assuming that you are selling a quality product), but to stress the value of your products/services, attach an affiliate action to the "test-drive". It may be a sign-up to your affiliate program and putting up one or two quality links on their website; or the "test-drive" may be attached to the first or second sale. If you are selling furniture, fireplaces, or any other bulky and expensive products or services (travel for example), neither the sign-up and activation, nor the first sale bonus structure will work for you. However, this does not mean that you should completely disregard this idea. Think further and I am confident you will be able to modify it to fit your context. Take this idea and make it conditional on your affiliate reaching a particular monetary amount in gross sales sent to you. For example, if you are in the travel vertical, you could be giving away roundtrip airfare tickets or trips for two. Just imagine what a promo that would be! Do the math, calculate what will work for you, and go for it.

Idea #19 – *Offer 100% Commissions*

Needless to say, promotions that have "100% commissions" in the title look attractive. If you are promoting an affiliate program for the manufacturer of a product or a direct supplier of a service (not a sub-contractor or reseller), such offers may be possible to run from time to time. They are especially great at the dawn of your program, when affiliates may not know the company or the product well and you want to make your program announcement have a strong impact. We did these for manufacturers of chewing gum and web-hosting suppliers, and I must admit they did pay off. Not only did we get many new sign-ups, but we also got plenty of activations and sales (i.e.: formerly-idle affiliates got their links up in an effort to achieve the goal).

You may offer 100% commissions on every second (or any other number) sale, sales above a particular number of sales within a set period (for example, all sales after the tenth one in the course of the current month), or even all sales within a period of time (for example, three days or a week). Do whatever you and the merchant deem reasonable and practical.

Idea #20 – *Run a "Free Graphics Help" Week*

If you feel it is feasible, you should run an ongoing graphics support campaign, providing your affiliates with banners of any size, shape, or color. However, I do understand that some affiliate programs may not have the resources to do this. If you do not, run at least one Free Graphics Help Week. At this time, you take in requests for any size banner (preferably unlimited number of banners per affiliate, as they will not ask you for banners they will not put to use immediately), promising to get the banners back to them within a set period of time. The reasoning behind this idea is as follows: affiliates may not be promoting you because the creatives you are supplying them with by default do not fit the spots they have assigned to merchant banners.

You are then losing potential sign-ups and also have those that are "on the list" (i.e. have joined the program), but cannot use the banners you are offering. Your goal during this week (again, it may be a month or any other period of time) is to get the stagnant affiliates supplied with the banners in sizes they need, and also to attract new affiliates by the offer.

Idea #21 – *Award "Every-Third-Sale" Gifts*

Do not take this literally. These gifts can be for every fourth sale, every fifth sale, etc. The idea is this: discuss with the merchant the thought of giving away gifts after every Xth sale (if you are working as an in-house affiliate manager, things may be simpler for you, because you will know the internal situation in the company). The idea may not be right for the merchant straight away, but when they are clearing all stock – be it after Christmas, another holiday, or just because they got in a new collection – this will be a great way to use the products. Explain it as an investment. You are not just giving away the merchant's products – you are essentially awarding gifts that, with the merchant's mark-up, cost them much less than they cost at the merchant's website. We ran this for one merchant as an Every Third Sale Gifts campaign, and announced the gifts given away as being worth $20+. The merchant did not really spend more than $7.50 on each of them, but a $20 gift is obviously accepted better than one that is only worth $7.50. It is a good way to stimulate sales, and it also allows the merchant to get rid of certain items. Additionally, it is an original way to award your affiliates. You are giving away $20 gifts instead of the $7.50 cash bonus that would basically be an equal deal for you (but not for the affiliate!).

Idea #22 – *Cash for Everything: CAI's, FSB's, etc.*

CAI stands for Cash Activation Incentive, while *FSB* is the First Sale Bonus abbreviation. It is a good idea to constantly run these for your program. They should be announced right in the first e-mail each affiliate gets from you – the approval e-mail. We have discussed these before (without abbreviating them), so I will not spend much time on them here. What I want to suggest is that every once in a while you run a "Cash for Everything" week. Such promotions obviously catch an amount of affiliate attention that can only be beaten by a 100% commission offer. During the "Cash for Everything" week, give away CAI's to those that haven't put their links up yet, FSB's, SSB's (second sale bonuses), and bonuses for every sale. You may synergize this idea with the arithmetic progression bonuses idea, and give away $5 for two links, $10 with the first sale, $15 on top of the second sale, and so on. The common difference does not have to be 5. It may be anything you want it to be. Also, you do not have to run such campaigns for a week. You may make it a one day, a three day (the absolute minimum I would recommend), or any other length campaign.

Idea #23 – *Cross-Program Promotions*

Cross-program promos work well both between programs managed by different affiliate managers, and between programs managed by one OPM. I have already referred to them while addressing the question of affiliate recruitment. Here I would simply like to give you two examples: (i) an example of a cross program promo between two programs managed by different affiliate managers, and (ii) an example of a promo an OPM/AM that manages several programs.

Between Programs Managed by Different AMs:

20% Cross-Program Commission Increase

It is our pleasure to announce our first- ever cross-program promotion, where every affiliate that generates a total of $499+ in sales between <Campaign Start Date> and <Campaign End Date> in both ours and <Company Name> affiliate program will get a 20% lifetime commission increase in both programs. For example, if you are on a commission level of 10%, we will raise it to 12% for you.

Important: Once granted, the commission increase will *also* apply to all sales generated between <Campaign Start Date> and <Campaign End Date>.

Between Programs Managed by one OPM/AM:

*5000th Sale = 100 * $50.00 Bonuses Cross-Program Promo*

To announce the 5000th affiliate sale received this year across all affiliate programs we manage, we would like to celebrate in a special way with all of our current and potential affiliates. We have 100 bonuses of $50.00 each (to make the total prize fund of $5000!!), and they will be given out in our Cross-Program Promotion Campaign. To get yours, generate $500 in sales in any of the following programs we manage:

<Program #1> <Respective Sign-Up URL>
<Program #2> <Respective Sign-Up URL>
<Program #3> <Respective Sign-Up URL>

Important:
(1) This promo is non-exclusive of all and/or any other promos run for the participating programs! The number of $50.00 checks to be given away is exactly 100, and this promotion

campaign is not limited by time (i.e.: we will run it until the last check is given out).

(2) The number of bonuses to be given out per affiliate is also unlimited. This means that the number of $50.00 checks you may receive is tied only to the number of $500 batches of sales you send for each of the above-quoted programs.

The numbers used in the above samples may be changed around to suit your own situation. The general idea of the first type of cross-program promo is to both encourage your affiliates to generate more sales, and to raise your affiliates' interest in another affiliate program. It is best if the two programs are somehow related. For example, if you are running a collectibles affiliate program, a good match would be a flower delivery program. If you are managing a gourmet products program, a kitchen utensils merchant with an affiliate program may very well be interested in running a cross-program promo with you. The second type of promo, on the other hand, aims at attracting affiliate attention to the full list of programs you manage. Both types of promos can have an excellent response if run at the right time and in the right manner.

Idea #24 – *Dynamic Scripts*

This idea is not new, but it should certainly be mentioned in a section such as this. The idea of creating scripts that let affiliates keep their websites up-to-date – without having to do much work on their end – always gives any affiliate program a considerable advantage in the face of its competitors. Such scripts may help affiliates import your whole inventory into their websites, or else choose what products to import. Some dynamic scripts may focus on your specials or price-drops only, while others may give affiliates a chance to display a dynamically updating list of the merchant's bestsellers right on the affiliate website. Having a good PHP programmer within a reachable distance will help your affiliate program satisfy the needs of your affiliates both quickly and efficiently. Do get a few dynamic scripts up for your program.

Idea #25 – *Commission-Beating Policy*

Do you see how online and offline merchants run price-matching and price-beating campaigns daily? Why not run an on-going commission-beating campaign for your own affiliate program? Here is how you can word it on the page with the description of your program:

a) Find an immediate competitor of ours that offers a better commission

b) Contact us at <Affiliate Manager E-mail>, present one of the following:

- URL with the advertised commission
- Screenshot of the base commission
- Email copy of commission offer
- Scanned copy of printed commission offer
- Description of a private offer (be prepared to provide proof)

c) We will beat the competitor's commission by 20%

You may offer a commission-beating pattern, or not specify the percentage by which you are going to beat the competitor's commission at all. It is up to you – but having it there makes your affiliate program look serious about the promise.

Before you offer this, analyze all possible ways how this could not work, and then make it work! Do your own competition analysis, and if it shows that certain merchants offer higher base commissions, analyze their prices and come up with a formula where you would still be offering your affiliates better conditions. Make sure you word your commission-beating proposal clearly, yet eloquently.

Idea #26 – *Exclusive Coupons for Select Affiliates*

This idea is not a new one either, but is definitely worth a mention. To begin with, all coupons offered to your affiliates should, by definition, be exclusive – not available anywhere but through your own marketing. No direct visitor of your website should be able to find these coupon codes; they should only be available through affiliate websites.

Exclusive coupons for select affiliates, on the other hand, implies creating private coupons and making their codes available/known only to the affiliate for which they were created. This technique works very well when you know to which affiliates you should offer such coupons. This is not an idea for public announcement, but with proper contacts in the affiliate world, it can help you give your program a very good acceleration.

Idea #27 – *Time-Sensitive Private Offers*

This is something we ran for one of our clients and it worked quite well. The idea was to make one announcement a week, targeting affiliates working in different spheres every week. The announcements were made via all methods available to us: our own database of affiliates, online affiliate forums, and the client's pool of affiliates (those that have already joined their program, but were not promoting it actively). The essence of each announcement constituted publicizing the merchant's intention to offer higher affiliate

186

payouts to those that work in specific areas. If you are selling backpacks, you would want to target affiliates with travel and sports traffic; if your product is gourmet foods, you would be interested in working with those affiliates that have holiday-related traffic, as well as those that are food-related. Make your offer time-sensitive, and *do not* announce exactly what you are willing to offer. Just ask them to contact you, letting you know where they can place your links, and assure them that they will not be disappointed by the offer. "Will not be disappointed" means a considerable commission increase. Make it worth their while. Do not offer 1-2% commission increases; a 50% increase is normally adequate to get them motivated.

Idea #28 – *Free Content Help*

When speaking of different types of affiliates, I have mentioned *content affiliates,* or those affiliates that that build content-saturated sites and feature merchants' banners, links and/or products on the side. Many of them are great writers of that content. They enjoy doing it, and what they write reads well and attracts visitors. However, not all affiliates have great writing skills. Some outsource copywriters can do the work for you. To save them the money and get them to prioritize your affiliate program's promotion over others, why not offer them free content help? By doing this, you will kill two birds with one stone: (a) you will provide them with the text they can use on their websites to promote your program "between the lines", and (b) you, yourself, will end up with a good selection of articles you could post around the Internet. It is a known fact that submission of articles to various e-zines and directories helps you with the search engine optimization of your own website. It is an excellent incentive for you to run a continuous "Free Content Help" campaign for your affiliates. Write one article a week and publish it on the Internet, giving your affiliates access to it, too. At the end of the year you will have 52 articles published all around the web, helping you with your search engine positions and also sending you visitors. In addition, you will have all of these articles available for affiliates to use on their websites.

<u>Important</u>: Do restrict your Content Help campaign by a condition that affiliates may only publish your articles at their *own* websites, so that you and your affiliates do not end up publishing them in the same online directories and e-zines.

Idea #29 – *Activation Incentives*

Affiliate activation is a topic that deserves special attention, as it is a well-known problem for every affiliate manager. I do not know of a single affiliate program that has at least *one-third* of all affiliates sending hits and sales. The reality is normally as dreadful as already mentioned in the foregoing – under one-sixth of all affiliates that any given program has on board are actively contributing to the life of the program. I have already mentioned over half a dozen methods that may be used to motivate your passive affiliates to "wake-up" (see the "What do I do with stagnant affiliates?" question). Here I would like to give practical examples of two activation incentives that I use daily: (i) cash giveaways, and (b) cookies and commission increases. *Cash giveaways* or bonuses presuppose immediate monetary remuneration for an action performed by an affiliate. You may give away cash for links put up on the affiliate website (smallest amounts), for data feed import (larger amounts), and/or on top of their first or second sale's commission (largest amounts). *Cookies & commission increases* may also be used as a powerful activation incentive tool. If your budget does not allow giving away cash bonuses right away, offer your affiliates cookies increases, commission increases, or a combination of both. Let me illustrate this by the way I do this for one of the merchants whose affiliate program I manage. Affiliates often request access to merchants' datafeeds. This is always a good sign, as it shows that they are planning on using the datafeed. However, experience shows that, just as with affiliate sign-ups, affiliate requests for datafeed access may not mean much unless you motivate them to get *active* with that datafeed. When I approve affiliates for datafeed access, I send each and every one of them a message that is worded along the following lines:

Dear <Affiliate's Name>

Congratulations! You have just been approved for FTP access to <Merchant's Name> datafeed.

Please let me know as soon as our products are up on your website.

PROPOSAL: If you add at least 1/2 of the datafeed to you website(s) by <Date, Month, Year>, we will raise your cookies life to 180 days. If you add at least 2/3rds, you will get 365 days cookies and an additional $10.00 bonus in your affiliate account.

Looking forward to hearing from you!

Best regards,

Geno
<Merchant's Name> Affiliate Manager

Once we introduced such datafeed approval e-mails, the number of affiliates that actually imported the datafeed into their websites raised from 8% to 47%. The effect was obvious, but it still left room for improvement. If you send out follow-up e-mails to those that never claim their activation "prizes", you will increase the effectiveness of your activation endeavors even more.

Idea #30 – *Turn A Sale Into A Contest*

In July of 2006, an affiliate sale came in through RussianLegacy's affiliate program. The sale was for $521.85. It was not your usual sale, though, as it consisted of a large number of one single product. All of a sudden, I was stricken by the words of Dr. Vernon A. Magnesen:

"We learn:

10% of what we read
20% of what we hear
30% of what we see
50% of what we see and hear
70% of what we say
90% of what we say and do"

90% of what is not only spoken, but also done, is remembered by the initiator of the speech and action. That is why I ran a contest two hours after this interesting sale came in. The conditions were simple:

We have just had the following sale come in:

<Printscreen of Affiliate Transaction> (with the sale amount and the large commission paid on it underlined)

Guess what was purchased, and get one of them yourself!

Within just 24 hours we had close to fifty guesses, and *none* of them hit the mark! Not one! The order was for 300 handpainted keychains (shaped like nesting dolls), and not one affiliate could guess it. Did it ruin the contest? Not at all. We achieved the higher goal: a large number of affiliates browsed the merchant's inventory of 3000+ products (that's your action), and voiced out their guesses (that's your speech). One of the affiliates admitted: "Smart idea, Geno. I never would have spent that much time digging through your site."

Appendix

Internet Marketing
Acronyms & Abbreviations

Below you will find a list of seventy acronyms and abbreviations with which every affiliate manager should be familiar. The list includes not only affiliate marketing shortenings, but also general marketing abbreviations that each affiliate manager should be comfortable using. We do not claim to have a complete list of acronyms and abbreviations, but this is a good basic one with which to start:

AD - Advertisement - May be in the form of a text, banner, flash, video or any other method that may be displayed on the Internet.

AM - Affiliate Manager - Person in charge of the management and organization of a company's affiliate program.

ASP - Active Server Pages - A Microsoft technology for dynamically-generated webpages that contain one or more scripts which are processed on a Microstoft web-server prior to the page being displayed to the end-user. The idea is somewhat similar to SSI (see below). See: www.asp.net

ASP - Application Service Provider - A third-party entity that distributes software applications or software-based services via a network or the Internet. Affiliate networks may be referred to as ASP's, as their features are accessible over the Internet by merchants and affiliates alike. While referring to affiliate networks "ASP" may also stand for the "affiliate solution provider".

B2B - Business to Business - A way of exchanging products or services *or* a transaction that takes place between businesses rather than between a business and a consumer.

B2C - Business to Consumer - A way of exchanging products or services *or* a transaction that takes place between a business and a consumer, rather than between one business and another.

BHO - Browser Helper Object - A DLL (see below) that allows its developers to customize and control the end-user's Internet Explorer. BHO's have access to all events and properties of each browsing session. Parasitic behavior is often closely associated with BHO's.

Bot - Robot - A software application that crawls the Internet with the purpose of indexing websites and webpages.

CAC - Customer Acquisition Cost - The cost associated with convincing a website visitor to become a customer for your product/service.

CB - Callback - A way of interviewing somebody after a product usage. The term may also refer to any repeated attempt to contact a potential responder after an unsuccessful first-contact attempt.

CGI - Common Gateway Interface - A way of transferring information between an Internet server and a CGI program. CGI programs are also often referred to as *scripts* and may be written in such programming languages as C, C++, Java and Perl.

CJ - Commission Junction Affiliate Network - One of the major affiliate networks nowadays. Has presence in the US, UK, Germany, France and Sweden. See: www.cj.com

CPA - Cost Per Action - Also sometimes de-abbreviated as Cost Per Acquisition, this is a payment model where an advertiser pays for each qualifying action made by the end-user in response to an Ad. Such qualifying actions normally fall into one of these categories: (i) sales, (ii) completions of registration or other website forms, confirming the end-user's interest in the advertiser's product/service.

CPC - Cost Per Click - A payment model where an advertiser pays for each click on an online Ad.

CPI - Cost Per Interview - General marketing term calculated as the full number of completed interviews divided by the budget allocated for the interviewing project.

CPL - Cost Per Lead - A payment model where an advertiser pays for each new qualifying lead. Examples of leads: (i) e-mail addresses, (ii) completed surveys, (iii) various online forms. This payment model is normally tied to the completeness and verification of the leads.

CPM - Cost Per Thousand - Cost per *mil* or one thousand impressions (or showings). May imply anything from the amount charged per 1000 banner impressions to a copy of a newsletter sent to 1000 subscribers.

CPO - Cost Per Order - A payment model where an advertiser pays for each new qualifying order.

CPS - Cost Per Sale - Total advertising expense divided by the total number of sales received as a result of such investment. The result of mathematical operation helps merchants determine the cost that has to be incurred to make each sale possible.

CR - Conversion Rate/Ratio - The percentage of visitors that take the desired action (purchase, subscription, form completion, etc).

CRA - Customer Relationship Analysis/Analytics - The processing of data about customers and their relationships with the merchant in order to improve the company's future sales/services and lower cost.

CRM - Customer Relationship Management - Improving customer service and general interaction with customers by means of relevant methodologies and software applications geared at bettering customer understanding, and increasing customer satisfaction and loyalty.

CSS - Cascading Style Sheets - A relatively new data format that, when added to HTML, helps separate style from structure. It gives both web-developers and end-users of websites more control over how webpages are displayed, and reduces HTML file sizes. Using CSS web-designers and end-users may create style sheets that determine how such elements as headers and links appear. The style sheets may then be applied to any webpage. *Cascading* refers to the fact that multiple style sheets may be applied to the same webpage.

CTR - Click-Through Rate/Ratio - A metrics used to measure response to advertising. CTR reflects the percentage of website visitors that click on a particular link. This percentage is obviously calculated based on the average number of click-throughs per 100 ad impressions.

DLL - Dynamic-Link Library - Defined by Microsoft as "an executable file that allows programs to share code and other resources necessary to perform particular tasks".

DPSC - Dynamic Product Showcase Creator - A tool created by AffSolutions that allows affiliates to generate a Javascript code which retrieves a merchant's product information that affiliates may then insert into their website. The code enables affiliate tracking and real-time updating of product information (AffSolutions also have static Product Showcase Creator for several merchants). This works only for merchants subscribed to this service. The full list of these merchants may be found at www.afftools.com/psc/directory.html

EPC - Earnings Per Click - Average affiliate program's payout per one hundred clicks. This metric is one of the key ones used by affiliates to determine how attractive and promising an affiliate program is. To calculate their EPC, affiliates divide the total number of clicks by their total earnings. Such simple calculation gives them their earnings per click.

EPM - Earning Per Thousand - Earnings per mil or one thousand link impressions.

FFA - Free-For-All (Link Lists) - Lists of hyperlinks where anyone can add a link back to their website, not having to abide by any qualifications.

IM - Instant messaging - A way of instant text communication between two or more people via an offline or an online-based application. IM may also stand for *Instant message* or an *Instant messenger*. The most popular instant messengers nowadays are: AIM (AOL instant messenger), YIM (Yahoo! instant messenger), MSN messenger, and one of the pioneers of the industry, ICQ. Skype has an IM imbedded in their application and allows not only for voice communication, but also for instant messaging in real time. Instant messengers are excellent for staying in touch with your affiliates worldwide.

LS - Linkshare Affiliate Network - One of the leading affiliate networks out there. See: www.linkshare.com

MLM - Multi-Level Marketing - A pyramid sales system within which salespeople not only receive commission on their own sales, but also smaller commission on the sales of the people they convince to become sellers. Such multi-tier programs are generally not welcomed in the affiliate marketing community (see "What about the second tier commission?" question above).

OPM - Outsourced Affiliate (Program) Manager - Affiliate manager that perform program management outside the company's premises. They are sometimes also abbreviated as OAMs or APMs.

ODP - Open Directory Project - The largest human edited directory on the Internet. Google and thousands of other websites are using its data throughout the web. Sometimes also referred to as DMOZ.

PFI - Pay For Inclusion - Also sometimes abbreviated as PPI (or Pay Per Inclusion), it is a search engine marketing model in which website owners pay a search engine to be listed in search results. Some search engines support it not distinguishing between paid listings and organically achieved search rankings, while others label PFI listings hidden advertising, demanding paid search results to be clearly marked as an ad.

PFP - Pay For Performance - An Internet marketing model based on delivering sales or other measurable performance.

PM - Private Message - An internal forum or other online community means of communication between the members of the forum/community.

POP - Point-Of-Purchase - The location where the product/service is actually purchased. May refer to both a physical location or to the online equivalent.

POS - Point-Of-Sale - Same as POP.

PPA - Pay Per Action - Another way to refer to a CPA model (see above).

PPC - Pay Per Click - An Internet marketing model in which website owners pay only for targeted clicks. When search engines' PPC campaigns are concerned, you pay only for clicks coming from searchers looking for the keywords that you bid on. The main providers of such model are Google (Google Adwords) and Yahoo! Marketing (Overture). The British Internet also has such large providers as Espotting.

PPCSE - Pay Per Click Search Engine - Search engine that supports PPC campaigns, allowing for the search results to be ranked according to the bid amount received. Advertisers are charged according to the classic PPC pattern – or only for the clicks occurred.

PPI - Pay Per Impression - An Internet marketing model in which payment is calculated based on the number of impressions an Ad receives.

PPL - Pay Per Lead - An Internet marketing model in which payment is due only when qualifying leads are received by the advertiser.

PPS - Pay Per Sale - An Internet marketing model in which payment is due only when qualifying sales are received by the advertiser/merchant.

PR - PageRank™ - Google's patented method for ranking webpages based on a complex technology (see: www.google.com/technology) that weighs each webpage on a numerical scale of 0 to 10. The purpose of such measuring consists in defining the relevance and importance of any given webpage within a set of the webpages it is hyperlinked with. Google's PR of a webpage has an immediate effect on organic ranking of the latter in search engines.

PSC - Product Showcase Creator - Static version of AffSolutions' DPSC (see the definition above).

PV - Pageview - There are two ways to define a pageview, depending on the context. One defines it as a single webpage viewed by a web-user through a browser. The other one characterizes every file which either has a text file suffix (.html, .text), or which is a directory index file as pageview. The latter definition helps estimate the number of authentic documents transmitted by the server, which is helpful for website statistics. Images, CGI scripts, Java applets, or any other HTML objects (except all files ending with one of the pre-defined pageview suffixes, such as .html or .text), are not considered pageviews.

ROI - Return On Investment - Originally a finance term, it reflects a measure of a company's profitability. It is equal to a fiscal year's income divided by common stock and preferred stock equity, plus long-term debt. In the investment and business analytics world, the ROI measures how effectively the investment is used to generate profit. In e-commerce, the term retains its financial sense, but more often than not, its definition is simplified to the evaluation of the money earned (or lost) against the amount of money invested.

RON - Run Of Network - An online advertising term that designates a type of Internet promotion where banners, images, media, or text ads appear on a network of websites.

ROS - Run Of Site - An online advertising term that is defined as a type of Internet promotion where banners, images, media, or text ads appear on a webpages within one website.

RSS - Real Simple Syndication *previously* Rich Site Summary - A file format originally developed by Netscape. On the one hand, it allows webmasters to put the content of their sites into a standardized format (an XML file called an RSS feed, webfeed, RSS stream or RSS channel); and, on the other hand, it lets users to subscribe to their favorite websites and view/ organize the content through RSS-aware software applications. As such, RSS provides a way for websites to dispense their content outside of a web browser. The RSS technology has basically provided the world with a better technique for users to automatically stay updated on their favorite websites. RSS supports news feeds, events listings, news stories, headlines, project updates, excerpts from online forums, and even corporate information.

SAS - Shareasale Affiliate Network - One of the leading present-day affiliate networks. Known for its stance against parasites, its strive for transparency, and strong affiliate support. See: www.shareasale.com

SE - Search Engine - A program developed to search for documents by keywords and key phrases. Each request returns a list of the documents where the requested keyword or key phrase is found. Examples: Google.com, Yahoo.com

SEM - Search Engine Marketing - Marketing acts associated with researching, submitting, and positioning a website within search engines with an aim at achieving the best website exposure on these search engines. The best exposure may be achieved by improving the website's search engine ranking, participating in PPC campaigns or a combination of these and other relative activities (for example, SEO).

SEMPO - Search Engine Marketing Professional Organization - A non-profit organization established to increase people's awareness of the value of search engine marketing through continuous education.

SEO - Search Engine Optimization - Acts associated with website altering with an aim of achieving higher website rankings on major search engines.

SEP - Search Engine Positioning - Acts aimed at achieving higher *organic* (natural) rankings on major search engines.

206

SERP - Search Engine Results Page - The page displayed to the end-user after submitting the search query.

SID - Shopper ID - A parameter that affiliates may add to their tracking URL's to be able to monitor which links produced which sales and/or leads. SID affiliate tracking was originally invented by Commission Junction (see www.cj.com/downloads/smartrewards.pdf), but it is now also offered by every major affiliate network, as well as by some providers of in-house software. The acronym is also sometimes spelled out as a *session ID*. I believe the time has come to broaden its meaning into a unified *Sub ID* which would include CJ's *sid*, DirectTrack's *dp*, LinkShare's *u1*, MyAffiliateProgram's *sub*, Performics' *mid*, ShareASale's *afftrack*, and other link parameters carrying out the same function.

SMB - Small and Medium-Sized Businesses - The abbreviation is used interchangeably with an SME shortening, which stands for small and medium enterprises. In the European Union, enterprises with fewer than 50 employees are categorized as "small", while those that employ fewer than 250 workers are considered "medium". In the United States, conversely, "small" businesses refer to those with fewer than 100 employees, while "medium" designates businesses with fewer than 500 persons employed. An interesting fact is that over 90% of all American businesses fall under the US definition of "small business".

SMOB - Small and Medium-Sized Online Businesses - An acronym created by us to designate small and medium online enterprises, as opposed to the online giants (such as Amazon, eBay and others).

SSI - Server-Side Include - A variable value (e.g.: a page "last updated" date) that a server can include in an HTML file before sending it to the end-user that browses the website.

SWOT - SWOT Analysis - A strategic planning tool aimed at singling out Strengths, Weaknesses, Opportunities and Threats in the object of study, arriving at an action plan for the proper use of the collected data. SWOT is an excellent way to analyze any marketing or management endeavor, affiliate programs included. The SWOT matrix essentially consists of four quadrants. Each of the quadrants helps the researcher analyze where the object of his/her study is now, where it is wanted to be, and how to get there (for details, see the "How can SWOT analysis help?" question and answer above).

TOS - Terms Of Service - Rules and regulations that one must agree to and follow in order to use a service. In the context of affiliate marketing, the TOS acronym is frequently used to designate either an affiliate program's agreement with affiliates, or an affiliate network's service agreement.

UBE - Unsolicited Bulk E-mail - E-mail messages sent to the recipient as a part of a larger group of messages, all of which have essentially identical content, and are sent out without prior recipient's permission. In short, UBE stands for e-mail spam. An e-mail message may be classified as spam only if it is *both* unsolicited and bulk. Not to be accused of UBE's, affiliate managers should be careful in the wording of the affiliate recruitment messages sent out (see the "How do I word my recruitment e-mail?" question and answer).

URL - Uniform Resource Locator - The global address of an Internet resource on the World Wide Web (e.g.: http://www.amnavivator.com)

208

UV - Unique Visitor - A term frequently used in tracking website's traffic, and designating a person that visits a website more than once within a specified period of time. Traffic tracking software normally distinguishes between visitors that only visit the website once, and UVs that return to the site. Unique visitors are different from hits or page views, both of which reflect the number of documents requested from the website. UVs are often determined by the number of unique IP addresses that the site visits come from.